Praying

FROM THE

Depths

OF THE

Psalms

John Henry Hanson, O. Praem.

Scepter

Published by Scepter Publishers, Inc.
info@scepterpublishers.org
www.scepterpublishers.org
800-322-8773
New York

Cover art: *The Annunciation* (1657) Nicolas Poussin / Alamy.com
Cover design: by StudioRed Design
Text design and pagination: by Rose Design

Library of Congress Cataloging-in-Publication Data available.

Names: Hanson, John Henry, author.
Title: Praying from the depths of the Psalms / John Henry Hanson, O.Praem.
Description: New York : Scepter Publishers, 2018.
Identifiers: LCCN 2018047690 (print) | LCCN 2018048711 (ebook) | ISBN
    9781594173448 (ebook) | ISBN 9781594173431 (pbk. : alk. paper)
Subjects: LCSH: Prayer--Christianity. | Bible. Psalms--Devotional use..
Classification: LCC BV210.3 (ebook) | LCC BV210.3 .H364 2018 (print) | DDC
    242/.5--dc23
LC record available at https://lccn.loc.gov/2018047690

ISBN: Paperback 9781594173431
ISBN: eBook 9781594173448

Special thanks to Elia Rivera, the St. Josemaría Institute, and Fr. Juan Velez of *www.cardinaljohnhenrynewman.com.*

Printed in the United States of America

Contents

Preface

This book is an invitation to prayer. In informed, prayerful, and graceful prose, Fr. John Henry Hanson draws us into the riches of the Psalms and invites us to feed on the Psalter as nourishment for our souls. His work is not primarily a commentary on, or scholarly exegesis of, a particular book of the Old Testament. Rather, as the author puts it, "The Psalter is the soul's hymnal. These are the songs of the soul's growing pains, its raptures, its confusion and distress, its agony and peace." The Psalms speak with us and for us—they express to God the joys, sufferings, anxieties, and exaltations of the human heart. They thereby teach us how to pray.

Fr. Hanson begins from the premise that all baptized Christians are called to a life of prayer, to a deep, interior life that seeks union with God in all circumstances and at every moment of the day. He understands that a Christian's personal prayer should be imbued with Scripture and informed by the Church's liturgy. The Psalms are a treasury of prayers not just for priests and religious who routinely pray the Divine Office, but for all the faithful—men and women, young and old, learned and simple alike. In the words of St. Gregory of Narek, as the author cites, "The Psalms were songs of everything for the pure in heart: a testament of life, written for all people." Like the Church herself, these prayers are universal.

The Psalms help us pray from within the heart of the Church, even in our "private" prayer. Praying the Psalms with the Church also means reading them with the saints and seeing them refracted through the lens of their lives. In this context, the author draws generously from the works of Augustine, Teresa of Avila, John of the Cross, John Henry Newman, and Josémaría Escriva, as well as modern spiritual writers such as Fulton Sheen and Hubert van Zeller.

More than a summary of common themes found in the Psalms, this book is a wise guide to the spiritual life—to the practice of praise, petition, thanksgiving, and remembrance of God's works in salvation history and in our own personal histories. There is much practical wisdom here. For example, Fr. Hanson shows us how memorized psalm verses can become habitual aspirations we recite at various moments throughout the day—or, as for the ancient monks, "'javelins,' to be hurled quickly and forcefully in the face of desperate trials and temptations."

In chapter seven, the author guides us to a deeper understanding of both God's mercy and our sin. The challenge is that "Remembrance of God's mercies often becomes a rival in a standoff against loitering memories of sin, shame, and regret." The author notes that, "Having our sins ever before our eyes is to do a balancing act between hope and despair." But with the help of Psalm 34, he assures us, "The heavenly throne is surrounded not by scores of shamefaced mortals, embarrassed to *be known*, humiliated that everyone knows everything about them. No, the shared feeling is enraptured amazement: 'O magnify the Lord with me, and let us exalt his name together!' (Ps 34:3)."

Those who begin to read the Psalms prayerfully might ask: What are Christians to make of the sometimes puzzling, even violent, language of the more "martial" psalms, which ask God not only for deliverance from enemies, but the destruction of enemies? Fr. Hanson explains, "Christian tradition has always seen the repeated cries of the psalmist for deliverance from his enemies not so much as a military conflict as a demonic one." In other words, our battles are not waged against worldly foes or human armies, but against principalities and powers, against the nefarious influence of the fallen angels who are intent on corrupting the human soul. In the Psalms, the tumultuous events of salvation history—the great dramas, the bloody battles won and lost—become a template for our own spiritual struggles.

Likewise, God's victory in salvation history outlines the pattern of our personal hope. Through praying the

Psalms, such as Psalm 114, God's past works become powerfully present for us today. "Regularly praying with the Psalms . . . sensitizes us to what God is doing in our lives, especially when his providence is not so easy to recognize." They make the central events of our salvation a tangible reality, leading us to sing a new song in celebration and thanksgiving. "Conditions change, cultures come and go, but the salvation of which we sing goes on."

Fr. Hanson provides keen insights on several themes relevant to the spiritual life. In chapter five, for example, he writes perceptively on the spiritual dangers posed by loneliness. In this context, he draws a helpful distinction between a soul-shrinking loneliness, which becomes a dead end if it does not lead to God, and a soul-expanding solitude, where we are turned toward the Lord, waiting on him, hoping in him, pleading with him for closer and deeper communion. "In the language of the Bible [solitude] comes across as hunger and thirst, as restlessness for the Lord."

On discernment of spirits, Fr. Hanson's advice contains much compacted wisdom, sketched in just a few lines:

> We can be insensitive to how God works in our lives because we lack the spiritual insight or discernment to pick out his handiwork from our own

impulses, temptations, or the illusions of the evil one. The movement of grace is always earmarked by the inspiration to humility, generosity, and joyful self-sacrifice. If we find ourselves sliding down the precipice into self-pity, rage, or bitterness, we would do well even to "force" ourselves to praise the Lord by slowly reciting a psalm such as 150.

This guide contains many other such gems of wisdom. The reader need only turn the page to begin the journey through the varied, challenging, and glorious terrain of the Psalms—always keeping in view the primacy of God's grace and the centrality of his mercy. It is our Lord who takes the initiative in every step of our spiritual progress: our salvation and sanctification are never a merely human endeavor, but always the work of God.

Aaron Kheriaty, MD
Author, *The Catholic Guide to Depression*

Introduction

At a Loss for Words

God has praised himself so that man might give him
fitting praise; because God chose to praise himself
man found the way in which to bless God.

—ST. AUGUSTINE[1]

Faced with overwhelming events or circumstances,
it's normal to be at a loss for words, whether we're
grappling with sudden tragedy or taking in an
unexpected joy. A sense of awe and wonder produces
speechlessness as intensely as a feeling of powerlessness
and defeat.

Sometimes that silence is itself a prayer, the most
fitting kind, in fact, when words seem only to get in
the way. The human inability to say the right thing
gives way to "sighs too deep for words," especially
when we seek to *pray through* profound sorrow or, on

---

1. Augustine, *Exposition of the Psalms*, 144.1, as quoted in Pius X,
Apostolic Constitution *Divino afflatu* (November 1, 1911). See *Liturgy of
the Hours*, vol. 4, p. 1336.

the other hand, "rejoice with unutterable and exalted joy" (cf. Rm 8:26; 1 Pt 1:8).

Since "we do not know how to pray as we ought," then in our weakness "the Spirit himself intercedes for us" in this nonverbal way (Rm 8:26). In fact, Jesus himself prayed in this way in his agony: "In the days of his flesh, Jesus offered up prayers and supplications, with loud cries and tears" (Heb 5:7).

Sometimes prayer is like that: a cry, a groan, a sigh. But not always. Most of the time our prayer fuses words and "sighs too deep for words." And nowhere do we find these better combined than in the Psalter of the Old Testament.

The Psalms give us words where our own words fail, helping us express the inexpressible. They furnish us with a kind of sacred vocabulary for praise, repentance, mourning, rejoicing—even giving voice to our feelings of betrayal, abandonment, and anger. No truly human emotion is off-limits in the Psalms. And if sometimes we feel spiritually tongue-tied before the Lord, the problem might be an underdeveloped taste for the very words he has already put into our mouths.

Comparing the psalms to a "mirror, in which the person using them can see himself," St. Athanasius sees in them a depth capable of reflecting "the stirrings" of our own hearts, as they are prayed "against the background of [our own] emotions."[2] *Owning* the inspired words and human sentiments of the Psalms is the key to praying them well. It is the difference between reading and praying them.

As St. Augustine implies above, God has given us words not only to bless and praise him, but also to express everything else before him. We can rejoice, mourn, complain, and so forth, in ways pleasing to God and healing for our souls. Whatever the occasion calls for, the Lord has provided us with words to sing, to ponder, to claim as our own.

Many fine commentaries on the Book of Psalms have already covered the ground of exegesis, from saints such as Augustine of Hippo, John Chrysostom, Thomas Aquinas, and Robert Bellarmine, to name only a few. These are well worth exploring, along with such contemporary commentaries as the Navarre Bible series.

Our scope here is more modest, and more personal. Taking the Psalms as they stand, as the inspired word of God,[3] and ourselves as we are, we will visit

---

2. St. Athanasius, *Letter to Marcellinus on the Interpretation of the Psalms*, as quoted in Pius X, Apostolic Constitution *Divino afflatu* (November 1, 1911). See *Liturgy of the Hours*, vol. 4, p. 1336.

3. We will set aside any historical-critical questions of authorship and assume mainly Davidic composition, where the Psalms give no other indication of origin (such as those attributed to King Solomon and Asaph, the chief liturgical minister of David's court).

the milestones where they meet us on our life's journey. Psalms stand as monuments along that journey, etched with the words of a fellow traveler—a close ancestor, a man after our own hearts. He has already been there, felt the feelings, and forged through the experience.

From Jewish Temple worship to the earliest Christian liturgical usage of the Psalms to the Responsorial Psalm of the contemporary Roman Mass, everyone with ears to hear and a tongue to sing finds his or her soul spoken for, understood, and lifted up by the Psalms of David. "In the Book of Psalms there is profit for all," says St. Ambrose of Milan, "with healing power for our salvation."[4]

St. Athanasius compares the books of Scripture to gardens, each producing its own special fruit. But "the Psalter is a garden which, besides its special fruit, grows also some of those of all the rest."[5] In a way, the Psalter is the compendium of the whole Bible.

---

4. Ambrose of Milan, *Explanations of the Psalms*, Ps. 1, 4.7–8: CSEL 64, 4–7, as quoted in the Liturgy of the Hours, vol. 3, Friday of the Tenth Week in Ordinary Time.

5. Athanasius, *Letter to Marcellinus on the Interpretation of the Psalms*, as quoted in *On the Incarnation*, trans. and ed. by a religious of CSMV (Crestwood, N.Y.: St. Vladimir's Seminary Press, 1996), p. 98.

As a Canon Regular, a religious priest of the Norbertine Order,[6] my life revolves around the Liturgy of
the Hours, the Choir Office, and the chanting of the
Psalms. Our order has as its main work the solemn celebration of the sacred liturgy and the praise of God in
choir. The Psalms are always on our lips. But our job
isn't done until we've allowed the verses to penetrate
our hearts, as St. Augustine instructs us in the Rule
we Norbertines follow: "Ponder in your hearts what
your lips are saying." It is my hope that these pages will
encourage the reader of the Psalms along this path of
contemplative pondering.

I often find myself coming to choir with questions and problems, hopes and aspirations, and yet
forgetting that the solutions I'm seeking are looking
at me from the pages of my Breviary, the Church's
collection of Psalms that makes up the Liturgy of the
Hours. If we will ponder in our hearts what our lips
are saying, we will find a divine voice coming out of
our own mouths.

Each of the following chapters offers a meditative
look into a psalm theme, not only as an aide to prayer,
but also as a guide to how we should read our own

---

6. The Norbertine Order (or Canons Regular of Prémontré, so
named after its first foundation in the French valley of Prémontré)
was founded by St. Norbert (1080–1134) in 1121.

lives, the highs and lows, and all that falls in between. St. Augustine of Hippo does just this in *Confessions*, his famous spiritual autobiography, offering in its first sentence the "keynote" of his life in two psalm verses:

> Great is the LORD, and greatly to be praised,
>   and his greatness is unsearchable. (Ps 145:3)

> Great is our LORD, and abundant in power;
>   his understanding is beyond measure. (Ps 147:5)

This great Doctor of the Church could think of no better way of introducing his life in Christ, including a long road to conversion and subsequent embracing of the monastic life, than by making the Psalms speak on his behalf.

I certainly have not exhausted all possible themes in these pages. In a sense, anyone who "meditates on the law of the Lord day and night" (cf. Ps 1:2) could write his or her own book on these or other themes. And that is the beauty of the Psalms: in speaking to and for all, they speak to each one of us differently. Under the Spirit's inspiration and guidance, the words match our needs of soul in every circumstance.

God calls us to live *in him*, and we can't afford to undergo any life experience "outside" of him, as though he were uninvolved or uninterested in our peaks and valleys. Not even our daily tedium is mere "filler" in the Christian life: "Christ is all, and in all" (Col 3:11).

If the Psalms impart nothing else, they teach us that God stands at the heart of every joy and suffering we experience. Sometimes it is only after we have cried out to him, in exaltation or dejection, that we see the figure of a King, a Shepherd, a Savior, rising from the valley of shadows as the lamp to our feet and the light to our path.

CHAPTER ONE

Out of the depths

The Ground Zero of Prayer

Deep calls to deep . . .

—PSALM 42:7

Hubert van Zeller, the great twentieth-century spiritual writer, once called attention to a danger in writing books about prayer. He cautioned that talking about something—even about prayer—can take the place of the thing itself. "Just as we can talk about prayer and not pray," he writes, "so in our prayer we can think about prayer and not pray."[1] This applies to many areas of life, from dieting and exercise to overcoming sin. We can talk all day and never make it to the starting line.

---

1. Hubert van Zeller, OSB, *We Sing While There's Voice Left* (New York: Sheed and Ward, 1951), p. 91.

The starting line or ground zero of prayer, particularly the prayer of the Psalms, is what Psalm 130 calls "the depths":

Out of the depths I cry to thee, O LORD!
Lord, hear my voice!
Let thy ears be attentive
to the voice of my supplications! (PSALM 130:1–2)

St. Gregory of Narek,[2] the most recently-named Doctor of the Church, describes this kind of prayer as "speaking with God from the depths of the heart." Few before or after this tenth-century Armenian monk have explored and mapped these depths as painstakingly as he. A glimpse into his approach to psalm prayer will show to what depths and heights our own prayer can go.

In titling this book *Praying from the Depths of the Psalms*, I am very deliberately evoking a line repeated throughout St. Gregory's famous prayer book, which

---

2. Gregory of Narek (or Narekatsi) (951–1003) was declared Doctor of the Church in 2015 by Pope Francis, ratifying not only the devotion of centuries of Armenian Christians, but also providing a vital introduction to a saint largely unknown to western Christians. The saint was further honored by the Holy Father in April 2018 with the installation of his statue in the Vatican Gardens.

he calls "a new book of Psalms."[3] At the outset of each of his searching meditations, St. Gregory reiterates as a keynote verse "Speaking with God from the depths of the heart." The line sets the tone for both author and reader of the meditations: going deeper into ourselves is indispensable if we would also go deeper into God. You can't have one depth without the other.

Listening to a saint's prayers from the depths opens us to the possibilities that prayer with God's own words offers us. Here we find St. Gregory making his own psalm of healing. As he exposes his wounds, he declares his own restoration:

> I who was broken, am restored,
> who was wretched, am triumphant,
> who was dissipated, am healed,
> who was desperately outlawed, find hope,
> who was condemned to death, find life,
> who was mortgaged by damnable deeds,
>   find the light,
> who was debauched by animal pleasures,
>   find heaven,

---

3. Gregory of Narek, *Speaking with God from the Depths of the Heart: The Armenian Prayer Book of St. Gregory of Narek*, trans. Thomas J. Samuelian, 4th ed., (Yerevan: Vem Press, 2015). A searchable online version is also available: *http://www.stgregoryofnarek.am*.

who was twice caught in scandal, again find
   salvation,
who was bound by sin, find the promise of rest,
who was shaken by incurable wounds,
find the salve of immortality,
who was wildly rebellious, find the reins
   of tranquility,
who was a renegade, find calling,
who was brazenly self-willed, find humility,
who was quarrelsome, find forgiveness.[4]

You can't expect to plumb the "depths of God" (1 Cor 2:10) unless you're willing to descend into the raw depths of self like the saints. Mystics such as the Carmelite St. Elizabeth of the Trinity[5] especially loved to read Psalm 42:7 ("Deep calls to deep") as this mutual calling:

> We must not, so to speak, stop at the surface, but enter ever deeper into the divine Being through recollection. . . . So must we descend daily this pathway of the Abyss which is God: let us slide down this slope in wholly loving confidence. "Abyss calls to abyss." It is there in the very depths

---

4. Narek, *Speaking with God*, Prayer 11E.

5. Canonized by Pope Francis, October 16, 2016.

> that the divine impact takes place, where the abyss
> of our nothingness encounters the Abyss of mercy,
> the immensity of the all of God.[6]

What St. Elizabeth of the Trinity calls "recollection" means an inner attentiveness to the Lord that convicts us of two inseparable truths: our poverty and God's greatness. Our personal poverty is the "depths" from which our truest and best prayer rises. This is where all deep prayer is born. To speak to God from the depths of the heart is to cry out from a place where we have nothing but nothingness itself to offer.

We live topside much of the time, *un*recollected, avoiding the depths, just dealing with the events of life as they come, but not living simultaneously in that secret inner chamber in which the Lord who *sees in secret* rewards us as only he can. Courageous souls willing to descend beneath the surface distractions, passions, and vanities of daily life will find themselves standing in the truth, before God.

Perhaps the finest description of the meeting that transpires between God and us in our depths, even in this life, is what Pope Benedict XVI wrote about the souls in Purgatory:

---

6. Elizabeth of the Trinity, "Heaven in Faith," in *The Complete Works: Major Spiritual Writings*, vol. 1 (Washington, D.C.: ICS Publications, 1984), p. 95.

Before his gaze all falsehood melts away. This encounter with him, as it burns us, transforms and frees us, allowing us to become truly ourselves. All that we build during our lives can prove to be mere straw, pure bluster, and it collapses. Yet in the pain of this encounter, when the impurity and sickness of our lives become evident to us, there lies salvation. His gaze, the touch of his heart heals us through an undeniably painful transformation "as through fire." But it is a blessed pain, in which the holy power of his love sears through us like a flame, enabling us to become totally ourselves and thus totally of God.[7]

At the heart's *ground zero*, no lies, charades, or masks are possible. All of our vices are denuded of the dressing that makes them seem respectable to us. There, we are nearest the original wound that cuts through our entire being, running like a fault line through so many of our desires and choices.

Praying from the depths of heart clearly isn't about straining the mind with thoughts, deep concentration, or even deep introspection. Allowing the grace of the Holy Spirit to well up within, to breathe as he wills, to intercede for us with groans beyond

---

7. Pope Benedict XVI, Encyclical on Christian Hope *Spe Salvi* (November 30, 2007), 47.

words, is to pray from the depths of the heart. Our humble openness to the truths he wishes to reveal, the sorrow he wishes to inspire, the joy he wishes to establish and increase, allows him to heal the soul from the ground up, so to speak.

Those who simply dabble in prayer may fail to see what all the fuss is about when people spend hours before the Blessed Sacrament or in the study of the Scriptures—a holy "time wasting" with the Lord, as Ven. Fulton Sheen called it.

For good reason does Psalm 34 invite and compel, "O taste and see that the LORD is good!" (Ps 34:8). You acquire a taste by *savoring* what you consume. And you can't acquire this unique spiritual taste without doing what saints and people of prayer do so much of: praying from the depths. Merely "saying" prayers is one thing, and a very good thing, but far from the best thing. To be a soul of deep prayer is to cry out like the one who waited in a lonely hollow until the Lord was ready to rescue him:

> I waited patiently for the LORD;
> > he inclined to me and heard my cry.
> He drew me up from the desolate pit,
> > out of the miry bog,
> and set my feet upon a rock,
> > making my steps secure.

As for me, I am poor and needy;
    but the Lord takes thought for me.
Thou art my help and my deliverer;
    do not tarry, O my God! (Ps 40:1–2, 17)

Praying from the depths does not simply mean that I won't try to save myself, as though I'm doing God a favor if I let him do it. It means I can't, and I know I can't. *I will wait patiently for the Lord*, and refuse to counterfeit his salvation by ducking into the escape hatches of sin— the self-indulgence of intoxication, lust, or tuning out reality with Internet and television. *I will wait patiently for the Lord, until he draws me from the desolate pit.*

Healthy diversion is one thing; substitution for salvation is another. It is one thing to get the mind off an unhealthy fixation by wholesome amusement, and another to counterfeit "the answer" to one's problem by numbing it. Major surgery is never fun but often necessary to eradicate a malady. The soul is no different. If the soul were shallow like a puddle, fingertips would go deep enough to clear it of its impurities. The human soul demands what Scripture calls "the hand of the Lord" or even "the arm of the Lord" to reach into depths that only the Lord can see.

Though I walk in the midst of trouble,
    thou dost preserve my life;

thou dost stretch out thy hand against the wrath
    of my enemies,
  and thy right hand delivers me.
The Lord will fulfil his purpose for me;
  thy steadfast love, O LORD, endures for ever.
  Do not forsake the work of thy hands.
  (Ps 138:7–8)

Salvation is the willingness to be carried by a Shepherd, rescued by a Redeemer, and pursued relentlessly by a Bridegroom. But I can't know my need fully unless I immerse myself in my own inner poverty. In quietly pondering myself in the mirror of the Psalms, I begin to grasp my need and the greatness of the salvation of my God.

In an age when technology both enables and expects "multitasking," blocking out time each day for one thing only may seem wasteful—even if it's the *one necessary thing*. We are used to combining activities for efficiency's sake; mixing cell phone conversations, texting, and so on, with just about every other activity is the order of the day. The idea of sitting quietly in God's presence, pondering a psalm, or making visits to the Blessed Sacrament might seem like pious add-ons to the really important stuff of my day. A luxury for monks and nuns, and nothing more.

But there is no way around it. We must risk feeling inefficient, unproductive, and even powerless for the sake of being still and knowing the Lord's nearness. Isn't this a quasi-command of Psalm 46: "Be still, and know that I am God" (v. 10)?

When the Israelites found themselves backed up against the Red Sea with Pharaoh in hot pursuit, Moses gave his terrified countrymen a similar counter-intuitive command:

> "Fear not, stand firm, and see the salvation of the LORD, which he will work for you today. . . . The LORD will fight for you, and you have only to be still." (CF. EX 14:13–14)

Once delivered and safe, Moses, his sister Miriam, and all the Israelites, sang something that could qualify as the proto-psalm, the first canticle of its kind in the Old Testament:

> "I will sing to the LORD, for he has triumphed gloriously;
>   the horse and his rider he has thrown into the sea.
> The LORD is my strength and my song,
>   and he has become my salvation;
> this is my God, and I will praise him,
>   my father's God, and I will exalt him.
> The LORD is a man of war;
>   the LORD is his name." (EX 15:1–3)

But they would never have had a song to sing, never have known the salvation of the Lord, had they not been willing to be vulnerable and patient and still. St. Thérèse exclaimed on one occasion: "It is so good to feel that one is weak and little!"[8] That's hard-earned trust and experience talking. Knowing it and feeling it are very different things. But when we move beyond the frontiers of theory and into the realm of experience, we know the Lord's faithfulness firsthand. Like the saints, we *get it*.

To be silent and listen to our own emptiness, to hear the disconcerting noise of inner conflicts and competing desires, like the thundering approach of Pharaoh's chariots, is to descend into our own depths. The Psalms are written to be prayed and sung from that place only.

---

8. Thérèse of Lisieux, *St. Thérèse of Lisieux: Her Last Conversations*, trans. John Clarke, OCD (Washington, D.C.: ICS, 1977), p. 74.

CHAPTER TWO

Praise

Our Eternal Vocation Begun in Time

Our thoughts in this present life ought to be centered on the praise of God, because to praise God will be our everlasting joy in the life to come, and no one will be fit for that future life unless he is well practiced in the art of praising God now.

—ST. AUGUSTINE[1]

Getting excited, applauding at concerts and movies, cheering and celebrating in sports and politics, all are second nature to us. And then there is God. There is the Blessed Trinity. And what do we do? The Psalms urge us: "Praise the Lord!" But do people any longer know how to praise the Lord?

---

1. Augustine, Exposition of Psalm 148, *The Works of Saint Augustine: A Translation for the 21st Century*, trans. and notes by Maria Boulding, OSB, ed. by Boniface Ramsey, part 3, vol. 20 (Hyde Park, New York: New City Press, 2004), p. 476.

"Praise is cheap today," writes Thomas Merton.

Everything is praised. Soap, beer, toothpaste, cloth-
ing, mouthwash, movie stars, all the latest gadgets
which are supposed to make life more comfortable—
everything is constantly being "praised." Praise is now
so overdone that everybody is sick of it, and since
everything is "praised" with the hollow enthusiasm of
a radio announcer, it turns out in the end that nothing is praised. Praise has become empty. Nobody
really wants to use it.[2]

What Father Merton observed more than half
a century ago has only ramped up over the last
decades. The in-your-face quality of images and slo-
gans programs us to be excitable and reactive, and
in the end, wearied. No wonder many people have
little interest or energy left over to praise God. The
Lord seems like just one more *thing* to applaud or
cheer. One even notices this tendency in some parish churches after Sunday liturgy—applause, almost
as though we don't know what to do with ourselves
once the Mass has ended. We are told to "go in
peace," but we can't.

---

2. Thomas Merton, *Praying the Psalms* (Collegeville, Minn.:
Liturgical Press, 1956), p. 10.

When I celebrate the Armenian Divine Liturgy, I am always impressed (and challenged) by the exchange between priest and people just prior to the final blessing. The people say or sing the words of Psalm 34:1: "I will bless the Lord at all times; his praise shall continually be in my mouth." But the question lingering in the air, along with the last traces of incense, is: *Will you? Will you really bless the Lord at all times? Will his praise really be always in your mouth?* Here is where we need to ponder in our hearts what our lips are saying.

St. Augustine takes his congregation to task on this very point. It's no small promise to say we will praise the Lord at all times; it means not only when times are good and prosperous, when we can identify good *as* good, but also when goodness is hidden from us. He is very blunt toward those who only praise God when his providence passes inspection:

> And so you praise God only as long as he confers benefits on you, and you are lying when you proclaim, *I will bless the LORD at all times; his praise shall be in my mouth always* (Ps 33:2 (34:1)). The song on your lips demands a like song from your heart, and you have sung in church, *I will bless the LORD at all times*. But how is this true *at all times*? If there is gain coming your way at all times, you

bless him all the time; but if things go wrong for you, you bless him no more, but curse.[3]

What St. Augustine teaches above about practicing the "art" of praise in this life makes us pause and think: What do we normally do with our thoughts and words and affections? Are they "centered on the praise of God"?

More than an expectation, it is our Christian vocation: "We who first hoped in Christ have been destined and appointed to live for the praise of his glory" (Eph 1:12).[4] Again, St. Paul encourages the first generation of Christians: "Let us continually offer up a sacrifice of praise to God, that is, the fruit of lips that acknowledge his name" (Heb 13:15).

How can we bless or praise the Lord continually, at all times?

To begin with, why do we praise anything at all? Simply put, we praise someone or something when we

---

3. Augustine, Exposition 2 of Psalm 48, *The Works of Saint Augustine: A Translation for the 21st Century*, trans. and notes by Maria Boulding, OSB, ed. by John Rotelle, OSA, part 3, vol. 16 (Hyde Park, New York: New City Press, 2004), p. 378.

4. Thomas Aquinas, *Commentary on St. Paul's Epistle to the Ephesians*, 1.4. St. Thomas Aquinas comments simply that St. Paul is speaking here of "the end of [our] predestination and vocation, namely, the praise of God."

recognize goodness in it. Even in the case of the over-done commercial praise mentioned by Father Merton, advertisers are drawing attention to a product's desirability, its goodness, however dubious or negligible it may be. Isn't *goodness* also why the Psalms tell us to praise the Lord?

> O give thanks to the LORD, for he is good;
>   his steadfast love endures for ever! (Ps 118:1)

But there is a problem here. If we're geared to enthusiastic praise of commercial goods, then praising the hidden God won't come easily to us who walk by faith, not by sight. Praise of God is not all about what we know or what we understand, much less about products that render life more comfortable. Praise is all about appreciating a goodness that we do not understand, because it is infinite and mysterious. Our Lord's paraphrase of Psalm 8:2 makes the point: "Out of the mouths of babes and sucklings thou hast brought perfect praise."[5] The clever and learned of this world, the sophisticated adults, have nothing to say, no song to sing.

Augustine, in fact, makes the same point:

> But who is it that blesses the Lord at all times, except the humble in heart. . . . What is it to be humble?

---

5. See Mt 21:15–16.

To not take praise unto [yourself]. Who would himself be praised, is proud: who is not proud, is humble. Would you not then be proud? That you may be
humble, say what is here written; "*In the Lord shall
my soul be praised: the humble shall hear thereof and be
glad.*" Those then who will not be praised in the Lord,
are not humble, but fierce, rough, lifted up, proud.[6]

The praise problem finds its solution in an active,
humble faith in God's personal, providential involve-
ment in our lives. When saints make sweeping state-
ments such as "everything is grace," they mean that
God is never absent but always alive and active and
involved with us, from the day's greatest moments
down to its nitty-gritty. That certainty makes the difference between offering a continual sacrifice of praise
or only the occasional word of thanks. This faith vision
separates the "artisans" of praise from the continually
rusty and awkward amateurs.

A compelling modern expression of this spirituality of praise comes from the recently canonized St.
Elizabeth of the Trinity, nun of the Dijon Carmel, a
contemporary of St. Thérèse who, like Thèrése, saw

---

6. Augustine, Exposition on Psalm 34 (33), *The Ennarations,*
or *Expositions on the Book of Psalms*, in *Nicene and Post-Nicene
Fathers: First Series*, vol. 8, p. 73. This public domain work can be
accessed at *www.newadvent.org*.

her vocation as bridging time and eternity. Harking back to Ephesians 1:12, Elizabeth claimed as her new name and vocation in heaven "*Laudem Gloriae*," the praise of the glory of God's grace.

But during her short twenty-six years on this earth, St. Elizabeth was already well practiced in her eternal vocation. For Elizabeth, *to praise the glory of his grace* meant allowing the Lord a completely free hand in touching her soul—moving, inspiring, purifying her, while also having her feel pain and suffering, particularly in suffering the ravages of Addison's disease. Everything that God willed would be done without objection, blockades, evasions—without any resistance whatsoever.

If you are the praise of the glory of his grace, you must be surrendered enough to let the grace flow into you and through you without hindrance. This is why St. Elizabeth connects grace and glory to obedience to God's will:

> A praise of glory is a soul that lives in God, that loves Him with a pure and disinterested love, without seeking itself in the sweetness of this love; that loves Him beyond all His gifts and even though it would not have received anything from Him, it desires the good of the Object thus loved. Now how do we effectively desire and will good to God if not in

accomplishing His will, since this will orders everything for His greater glory? Thus the soul must surrender itself to this will completely, passionately, so
as to will nothing else but what God wills.[7]

To be a *praise of the glory* of God's grace, you must
concretely believe that God's will is good, not just in
theory, but in the way you actually think and act. And
if, as Elizabeth says, a praise of glory "is one who is
always giving thanks,"[8] this divine will must be the
ultimate motive of thanksgiving.

I must go through each day, receiving everything
that comes my way, as coming from the hands of a good
God—the God who knew me before he formed me in
my mother's womb, the God who calls me by name
and says, "You are mine." It is this God and no other
who must be Lord of my life, and Lord of my day.

If I see God's will only occasionally, then in the
meantime I'm going to interpret a lot of events as mistakes, maybe a hiatus, maybe just as random happenings.
No good for us to go through life praising the Lord only
when things are clear: "I will praise the Lord *at all times*."

It might help to consider the vantage point of a
former atheist. C.S. Lewis, the famed scholar and

---

7. Elizabeth of the Trinity, "Heaven in Faith," in *The Complete
Works*, p. 112.

8. Ibid.

Christian apologist, recalls a time in his life when if someone had asked him if this world is "the work of a benevolent and omnipotent spirit," he would have replied that "all the evidence points in the opposite direction. Either there is no spirit behind the universe, or else a spirit indifferent to good and evil, or else an evil spirit."[9]

Yet Lewis pauses on a question that never entered his head as a convinced atheist, but that also demanded fair treatment.

> There was one question which I never dreamed of raising. I never noticed that the very strength and facility of the pessimists' case at once poses us a problem. If the universe is so bad, or even half so bad, how on earth did human beings ever come to attribute it to the activity of a wise and good Creator? Men are fools, perhaps; but hardly so foolish as that.[10]

People aren't so "stupid" as to continue calling God good if their experience has consistently been the opposite. No one is as sentimental, blind, or self-deceived as that. If no higher Being was listening to the cries of the poor and suffering, people would

9. C.S. Lewis, *The Problem of Pain* (San Francisco: Harper Collins, 2001), p. 3.

10. Lewis.

long ago have fallen silent. But they haven't, and apparently can't.

This tells us that praise of God is truly praise of a providence incomprehensible to us, involving suffering and inexplicable tragedies, combined with times of surpassing joy and glory. Our God is a hidden God, acting in quiet and subtle ways, not extinguishing the smoldering wick or bruising the damaged reed. Praise must come from souls so fine-tuned as to pick up the divine frequency.

> The LORD is near to all who call upon him,
>> to all who call upon him in truth.
> He fulfils the desire of all who fear him,
>> he also hears their cry, and saves them.
> The LORD preserves all who love him;
>> but all the wicked he will destroy.
>
> My mouth will speak the praise of the LORD,
>> and let all flesh bless his holy name for ever
>>> and ever. (Ps 145:18–21)

I think praise brings healing to the soul in a unique way, healing any resentment or bitterness that may accumulate over time. No matter how bad things may be, or have been, or might be, there is always more good than bad present, if only we have eyes to see it! If saints like St. Maximilian Kolbe could find and serve

God in prisons and concentration camps, can't we do the same in the imperfect circumstances of life? St. Maximilian Kolbe, in fact, led his fellow inmates in hymns and songs of praise in the starvation bunker in which they all eventually perished.

This reveals another potent facet of praise. Praise not only heals, not only anchors us in the reality of God's presence, but also upholds the soul during its earthly pilgrimage, as St. Leo the Great wisely attests:

> Nothing more sustains and strengthens Christian souls, the devout disciples of peace and truth, than persevering and unwearied praise of God, saying with the Apostle: "Always rejoice, pray without ceasing. In all things give thanks; for this is the will of God in Christ Jesus concerning you all" (1 Thess 5:16–18).[11]

The alternative to praise, to choosing to praise God no matter how we feel, is a debilitating and self-defeating round of criticism and resentment. *My life hasn't turned out the way I thought it would. I'm not satisfied with this or that. My expectations and demands have not been met.*

The ability to see how God's grace is reaching into our lives in humble but continual ways determines

---

11. Leo the Great, *Homily 21* (PG 12), as quoted in *The Sunday Sermons of the Great Fathers*, vol. 1 (Chicago: Henry Regnery, 1957), p. 81.

whether or not we will praise him for his grace. We can be insensitive to how God works in our lives because we lack the spiritual insight or discernment to pick out his handiwork from our own impulses, temptations, or the illusions of the evil one. The movement of grace is always marked by the inspiration to humility, generosity, and joyful self-sacrifice. If we find ourselves sliding down the precipice into self-pity, rage, or bitterness, we would do well even to "force" ourselves to praise the Lord by slowly reciting a psalm such as 150:

> Praise the LORD!
> Praise God in his sanctuary;
>   praise him in his mighty firmament!
> Praise him for his mighty deeds;
>   praise him according to his exceeding greatness!
>
> Praise him with trumpet sound;
>   praise him with lute and harp!
> Praise him with timbrel and dance;
>   praise him with strings and pipe!
> Praise him with sounding cymbals;
>   praise him with loud clashing cymbals!
> Let everything that breathes praise the LORD!
> Praise the LORD!

Although we praise what we do not completely understand, God's grace and mercy are not unknown to us. Haven't good changes taken place in our lives that we clearly didn't make happen by snapping our fingers? Haven't we met and overcome struggles? Haven't we suffered, and yet recognized a gentle presence accompanying us in our tears?

We can look at our moral and spiritual struggles and ask: How could God love me and give himself up for me? How could God go on loving me when I have failed him so often? When my mind struggles to hold onto a single good thought, how is it that he doesn't lose patience with me? Or when I get excited about all the wrong things? I do not know. I do not understand. Instead: I praise the Lord. I am compelled to praise the Lord. Like the prophet Jeremiah, there is *a fire in my bones*, and I cannot hold it in.

I must give thanks and praise.

CHAPTER THREE

Penitence

Repenting with Hope and Joy

> Sorrow for sin is indeed necessary, but it should not be an endless preoccupation. You must dwell also on the glad remembrance of God's loving kindness . . .
>
> —St. Bernard of Clairvaux[1]

J oining repentance with rejoicing and having hope while sitting beside Job on the dunghill of sorrow or contrition sound more like mismatched marriages than ones made in heaven. But in reality, no one can be truly repentant, truly sorry for past sins, unless that sorrow finds close companions in joy and hope. If God calls us to the heights of holiness, then even slight turbulence is enough to throw us off course—not off the path of perfection altogether, but to deflate

---

1. Bernard of Clairvaux, *Sermons on the Song of Songs*, vol. 1 (Kalamazoo, Mich.: Cistercian Publications, 1971), p. 70.

the hope needed to stay buoyant amid the dips in our moral life. Those who seriously try to imitate and follow Christ, who aim high in the spiritual life, always run the risk of either *falling low* or *feeling low* when they fail. And nothing so poisons Christian effort as unchristian despair. St. Bernard completes his above thought with the same idea: "sadness will harden the heart and lead it more deeply into despair."[2]

Scripture tells us to have sorrow for sin, but warns about going to excess: "For sorrow results in death, and sorrow of heart saps one's strength" (Sir 38:18).

There is a difference between holy grief that leads to life and a sorrow that debilitates:

> I rejoice, not because you were grieved, but because you were grieved into repenting; for you felt a godly grief, so that you suffered no loss through us. For godly grief produces a repentance that leads to salvation and brings no regret, but worldly grief produces death. (2 Cor 7:9–10)

Everyone knows the drain attending deep grief over the loss of loved ones. But the sorrow that joins hands with repentance must be different. While it too "drains" the soul, God replaces the emptiness with hope,

---

2. Bernard of Clairvaux, p. 70.

promising recovery of what was lost, life where spiritual death had reigned. If the Parable of the Prodigal Son teaches us nothing else, it shows us the joy-giving nature of repentance in God's eyes.[3] The finest robe, family ring, and sandals indicate reinstatement in the family—recovery, welcome, and encouragement for the future. Where you expected punishment, a party is thrown in your honor.

The Psalms are our God-given script for right repentance, with contrition always wedded to hope.

> Restore to me the joy of thy salvation,
>> and uphold me with a willing spirit.
>
> Then I will teach transgressors thy ways,
>> and sinners will return to thee. (Ps 51:12–13)
>
> And now, Lord, for what do I wait?
>> My hope is in thee.
> Deliver me from all my transgressions. (Ps 39:7–8)
>
> Why are you cast down, O my soul,
>> and why are you disquieted within me?
> Hope in God; for I shall again praise him,
>> my help and my God. (Ps 42:5–6)

---

3. See Luke 15:11–32.

O God, thou knowest my folly;
>   the wrongs I have done are not hidden from thee.

Let not those who hope in thee be put to shame
>   through me,
>   O Lord God of hosts;
let not those who seek thee be brought to
>   dishonor through me,
>   O God of Israel. (Ps 69:5–6)

This sampling shows two inseparable things: total honesty about your state of soul—sinful, depressed, ashamed—joined to indefatigable confidence that God not only *can* but *wants* to pull you out of this state. Without at least that much faith, you'll stay stuck in the mire the psalmist begs to be delivered from: "I sink in deep mire, where there is no foothold" (Ps 69:2).

One of the keys to psalm prayer is not only taking the words on your lips, but allowing the spirit of trust and confidence to penetrate the heart. No matter how bad things get for him, the psalmist cannot suppress a final confident cry for rescue:

O my God, I cry by day, but thou dost not answer;
>   and by night, but find no rest.

Yet thou art holy,
>   enthroned on the praises of Israel.

In thee our fathers trusted;

    they trusted, and thou didst deliver them.

To thee they cried, and were saved;

    in thee they trusted, and were not disappointed.
(Ps 22:2–5)

The wisdom of the psalmist, though, submits all desire for deliverance to God's time:

At an acceptable time, O God,

    in the abundance of thy steadfast love answer me.

With thy faithful help rescue me

    from sinking in the mire;

let me be delivered from my enemies

    and from the deep waters. (Ps 69:13–14)

This willingness to wait for an "acceptable time" points to a crucial attitude for successful prayer, an attitude we often neglect in times of distress and need. All good prayer keeps God's will steadily in its sights. We pray either to know his will, praise his will, or surrender to it in difficult times. In the end, it all comes to the same thing: "Thy will be done, on earth as it is in heaven."

When people laboring under the burden of sinful habits reach a breaking point, where they've had enough, impatience to get rid of their vice is normal. But often God doesn't seem to be in as much of a hurry.

Does this seem strange? As we experience repeated falls, one step up and two steps back, the jagged edge of spiritual and moral progress perplexes us.

But God permits our return journey to him to be uneven for a very important reason. If we are honest, we might admit that our wish to be rid of a particular sin amounts to wanting to save ourselves from embarrassing or humiliating problems, so that we won't feel ashamed of ourselves. Fair enough.

But the more important lesson in God's eyes is that we learn to depend radically on a Savior, learning to trust him not simply more than ourselves, but *instead of* ourselves. This is just another way of saying that salvation comes by grace, not by our own strength. Didn't St. Paul struggle with the very same phenomenon? Distressed by the persistence of a "thorn" in his flesh, he begged the Lord three times for deliverance. The Lord's reply? "My grace is sufficient for you, for my power is made perfect in weakness." And St. Paul responds not with annoyance or resentment, but with the wisdom of a humbled sinner: "I will all the more gladly boast of my weaknesses, that the power of Christ may rest upon me" (2 Cor 12:9).

People find power intoxicating—political power, spending power, physical power, access to powerful people and things, and so on. More than a few spiritual books exist with "power" in the title. All of this is an appeal to our dislike for weakness and desire for transformation: we want to tap into strength that can change us. Valuing power and strength is clearly not wrong. But it is spiritually deadly to seek them apart from God.

The story of ongoing idolatry in the Old Testament is really a history of man's dark desire for demonic assistance in getting power over himself, others, nature, and material things. The "graven" images of pagan gods and goddesses were nothing more than symbols of the things that fallen people covet most: power, wealth, military conquest, and sexual indulgence. When these get a grip on the soul, the process of turning back to God makes one feel completely at the mercy of "the powers, . . . the world rulers of this present darkness, . . . the spiritual hosts of wickedness" (cf. Eph 6:12).

But "by the strength which God supplies" (1 Pt 4:11) is the motto of the recovering sinner, the saint in-the-making. Or among the Psalter's numerous invocations to God as "my strength":

> The LORD is my strength and my shield;
>   in him my heart trusts;
> so I am helped, and my heart exults,
>   and with my song I give thanks to him. (Ps 28:7)

If, as St. Josemaría tells us, "Our Lord wants us to rely on him for everything,"[4] then we ourselves need to be convinced of our need for such radical dependence. It must be "glaringly evident to us that without him we can do nothing, whereas with him we can do all things."[5]

St. Augustine of Hippo (354–430), whose conversion to Christianity is arguably second in importance only to St. Paul's, writes in his spiritual autobiography that "My whole hope is only in Thy exceeding great mercy."[6] Augustine had lived the first part of his adult life seeking his fame and fortune as a teacher of rhetoric, while keeping a mistress or two on the side, eventually fathering a child out of wedlock. He knew firsthand the struggle to be both humble and pure, and even described his difficult turning from a life of sin as a warfare, as a mighty storm raging in his breast.

So when he arrives at God's mercy as his only hope, he speaks not from the vantage point of a theoretician, but of a rescued man. A drowning man pulled out of a tempestuous sea and set on the firm deck of a rescue boat would speak in exactly the same way. Trembling

4. Josemaría Escrivá, *Friends of God* (New York: Scepter, 2002), no. 305.

5. Escrivá.

6. Augustine, *Confessions*, 10.29.40.

and terrified, but relieved, he would know without doubt where his "salvation" came from.[7]

Augustine learned not only to believe in the idea of a Savior, but to cleave to him with his entire being. Experience taught him not to trust in self or in the world, but in the unchanging Lord:

> My evil sorrows contend with my good joys; and on which side the victory may be I know not. Woe is me! Lord, have pity on me. Woe is me! Lo, I hide not my wounds; Thou art the Physician, I the sick; Thou merciful, I miserable. Is not the life of man upon earth a temptation?[8]

When we ask ourselves what holds us back in our spiritual lives, we should carefully avoid isolating one thing and setting it up as *everything*: my problem, my sin, my issue, the obstacle I trip over all the time. It's true, when we examine our conscience there's usually

---

7. I cannot omit mentioning a particularly poignant gesture made by St. Augustine in his final illness. According to his earliest biographer, Augustine wished that the Seven Penitential Psalms of David be posted on the wall opposite his bed as he lay dying, because he believed that "after receiving baptism even exemplary Christians and bishops should not depart this life without having repented worthily and adequately." *Life of St. Augustine* by Possidius, Ch. 31. These seven traditional Psalms of repentance are Psalms 6, 32, 38, 51, 102, 130, and 143.

8. Augustine, *Confessions*, 10.28–29.

one thing that looms large: *It's this bad habit that I've been struggling with for years. I can't get the tiger by the tail. And I can't move forward until it's gone.*

The Gospel tells us a different story about ourselves, different from the one we often narrate to ourselves. We see Jesus fully prepared to get involved with people in their sinfulness, whether in the heat of struggle or in the shame of defeat. But he doesn't enter our lives to fix our problems and then move on. Jesus is not a repair man! He is the Redeemer. Redemption means more than buying each of us back from a bad life; it means restoration. And what needs to be restored most in every human soul without exception is trust in God.

> And those who know thy name put their trust
>   in thee,
>   for thou, O Lord, hast not forsaken those
>   who seek thee. (Ps 9:10)

What often drives people to seek the Lord, sometimes as a last resort, is that one unshakable difficulty without which we think all would be well. When the struggle makes us feel forsaken and alone, it is in receiving the Lord's help that trust is restored.

Our lack of trust has deep roots. Adam and Eve fell because of pride, but the devil couched his temptation in the language of distrust. Did God tell them they couldn't eat of any tree in the garden? No, just one, and under pain of death. But the serpent claims to have the inside scoop:

> But the serpent said to the woman, "You will not die. For God knows that when you eat of it your eyes will be opened, and you will be like God, knowing good and evil." (Gn 3:4–5)

In other words, God can't be trusted. And we, the poor, banished children of our first parents, have inherited the original distrust that makes us want to save ourselves. The Psalms show us what so many saints and sinners have discovered through the hard knocks of personal weakness:

> Save me, O God!
> For the waters have come up to my neck.
> I have come into deep waters,
>   and the flood sweeps over me.
> I am weary with my crying;
>   my throat is parched.
> My eyes grow dim
>   with waiting for my God.
>
> I am afflicted and in pain;
>   let thy salvation, O God, set me on high!

I will praise the name of God with a song;
>   I will magnify him with thanksgiving.
Let the oppressed see it and be glad;
>   you who seek God, let your hearts revive.
For the LORD hears the needy,
>   and does not despise his own that are in bonds.
>   (CF. Ps 69: 1–3, 29–33)

There is more to conversion and repentance than breaking a bad habit and building a virtue. The whole process of breaking away from sin—and addictions, for that matter—means transferring our dependence from sin to God. Sin is certainly a kind of crutch that props up lack of self-esteem, allows pride to assert itself, and gives questionable pleasures free reign. In practice, this conversion means turning into the little children whom Jesus says we must become if we want a place beside him in the kingdom (cf. Mt 18:1–4).

This is exactly where we need to imitate the resilience featured in the Psalms and in the lives of the saints. The easiest thing for fallen people to do is, not surprisingly, to stay down after a fall. And what keeps us down is the oppressive thought that getting up again won't make any difference. We've been down before, gotten up again and again with wobbly legs, and ended up back where we started.

God's goodness accommodates a generous margin of error. Our clumsy missteps, our sour notes, can be incorporated into a harmony that only the divine mind can foresee and orchestrate. Like a virtuoso's intentional mistake that displays an unexpected expertise, the glory comes not from the error but from the one who reworks it into a fitting piece.

At the end of the day, tolerating weaknesses, failures, and mistakes is more valuable than we may think, as St. Josemaría Escrivá explains:

> As we walk along it is inevitable that we will raise dust; we are creatures and full of defects. I would almost say that we will always *need* defects. They are the shadow which shows up the light of God's grace and our resolve to respond to God's kindness.[9]

God does not bless human sin, but he is more than willing to pick up children who try and fail. In fact, the psalmist shows us in a particularly tender image where we arrive at the end of this journey of conversion. We end up at our own starting place, our mother's breast, but having acquired the wisdom to know why we're there:

---

9. Josemaría Escrivá, *Christ is Passing By* (New York: Scepter, 2002), no. 76.

O LORD, my heart is not lifted up,
　　my eyes are not raised too high;
I do not occupy myself with things
　　too great and too marvelous for me.
But I have calmed and quieted my soul,
　　like a child quieted at its mother's breast;
　　like a child that is quieted is my soul.

O Israel, hope in the LORD
　　from this time forth and for evermore. (Ps 131)

To be as little children—who know how to fail, stand up, and carry on—is so essential to our salvation that the Lord leaves us with defects, even with the ability to sin, so that we will learn to accept our more important need for dependence: to trust in God both for forgiveness and strength. If St. Paul astounds us with his paradox, "when I am weak, then am I strong" (2 Cor 12:10), he also emboldens us to claim as daringly: "And when I am most childlike, then am I most mature."

CHAPTER FOUR

The Valley of Shadows

Suffering beside the Shepherd

People react to suffering in different ways. But almost always the individual enters suffering with a typically human protest and with the question "why."

—St. John Paul II[1]

God wills that suffering be a significant, that is, a *meaningful,* part of our lives. And he calls us not merely to cope with this as an unavoidable fact but to receive it even as a gift, a saving grace. "It is good for me that I was afflicted," are the incredible-sounding words of Psalm 119:71, revealing a wisdom gained only from experience, but not simply the experience of suffering. It is suffering in union with, or accompanied by, the Savior.

---

1. John Paul II, Apostolic Letter on the Christian Meaning of Human Suffering *Salvifici doloris* (February 11, 1984), 26; emphasis in original removed.

I know, O LORD, that thy judgments are right;
  and that in faithfulness thou hast afflicted me.
Let thy steadfast love be ready to comfort me
  according to thy promise to thy servant.
Let thy mercy come to me, that I may live;
  for thy law is my delight. (Ps 119:75–77)

I'm not sure if there exists a wider gap in the Christian life than the gulf between "suffering theory" and actual suffering. Christians recognize value in suffering because of the redemptive sufferings of Christ. "Provided we suffer with him" (Rm 8:17) is the condition St. Paul lays down for our being coheirs with Christ and future sharers of his glory. His wounds mysteriously but truly invest ours with incalculable worth. If you've ever prayed before a crucifix and felt understood and consoled, then you've intuited this connection between Jesus in his passion and your own sufferings.

But the time inevitably comes when personal suffering goes beyond anything we could have imagined or prepared. And at those times, anything said by way of consolation, however well intentioned, tends to sound hollow. No human words can really reach the core of our pain. In fact, when grief is too devastating all most of us can do is to *feel* a numbing anguish that darkens the mind and depresses the heart.

Father Jesús Urteaga starkly depicts the distressing loneliness that suffering imposes, but not before pointing us to safe haven:

> Sooner or later you will become very much aware that "God alone . . . is my rock and my salvation, my fortress" (Ps 62:5–6); for in times of deep suffering, all else fails. Advice sounds like mockery, and pity is a painful hammering which drives the steel nails even deeper into your hands and feet.[2]

The wisest approach to the "deep suffering" Fr. Urteaga describes actually takes place in times of tranquility, in the absence of pain. Times of distress are too fraught with feeling for us to think straight, and we naturally fall back on what we know best, what we're used to. We cope with the equipment we have at hand. Although knowing the Lord and his ways isn't an inoculation against suffering, it provides an inspired framework, a perspective, without which we are untethered ships.

The best course is to live always in a state of preparation not trepidation, which is looking out for disaster and doom. Rather, ever prepared, to embrace God's will whatever it might entail.

---

2. Jesús Urteaga, *Saints in the World*, 3rd ed. (Princeton: Scepter, 1997), p. 122.

> For thou, O God, hast proved us: thou hast tried
>   us by fire, as silver is tried.
> Thou hast brought us into a net, thou hast laid
>   afflictions on our back:
> thou hast set men over our heads.
> We have passed through fire and water, and thou
>   hast brought us out into a refreshment.
>   (Ps 65/66:10–12)[3]

Knowing ahead of time that the Lord brings even his friends "through fire and water" helps us anticipate the promised pasture of refreshment. Any dark tunnel may be endured if the hope of daylight beckons us, even faintly, on the other end. Again, we are promised no exemption against suffering, but rather given the tools with which to suffer well, in ways that bring growth and bear fruit.

Evidence of the inevitability of deep human pain is nowhere more poignantly registered than in St. John's Gospel when Jesus is described twice as "deeply moved in spirit and troubled" (Jn 11:33–38). At the heart of a scene of distress, Jesus weeps at the tomb of his friend, Lazarus, from a depth of feeling only God can experience and fathom.

---

3. Douay-Rheims version.

So potent is this kind of anguish for us that the psalmist finds himself resisting consolation, unable to sleep, and practically speechless:

> I cry aloud to God,
>   aloud to God, that he may hear me.
> In the day of my trouble I seek the Lord;
>   in the night my hand is stretched out without
>   wearying;
>   my soul refuses to be comforted.
>
> I think of God, and I moan;
>   I meditate, and my spirit faints.
> Thou dost hold my eyelids from closing;
>   I am so troubled that I cannot speak. (Ps 77:1–4)

How do you counsel someone in this state of mind? If the sufferer himself can barely articulate his anguish, can an "outsider" dare to intrude with his or her own words?

One of the most difficult questions asked of priests comes from those treading this path through the valley of shadows: "Why did God let this happen?" or "Why didn't God prevent that from happening?" The death or abuse of a child, a brutal attack, terminal disease (especially in the young), divorce. There is almost no end to the tale of human woes compelling us to ask, "Why?"

The worst thing people can do is to fault themselves for their own God-given instincts—the sadness or anger arising from tragic or difficult circumstances. The questions are not at all wrong or impious to ask, but spontaneous and natural. St. John Paul II hearteningly comments that although in our "dismay and anxiety" we inevitably question why we suffer, "God expects the question and listens to it."[4]

It's important to know what's happening here. If we don't handle our wild thoughts and emotions with faith, we won't see the purpose behind what God permits or prevents in our lives. Quite honestly, the questions are really the beginning of a dialogue we never would have wanted to initiate. Listen to the voice of the psalmist speaking in the person of the Messiah embarking on this difficult and disturbing exchange:

My God, my God, why hast thou forsaken me?
Why art thou so far from helping me, from the words of my groaning? (Ps 22:1)

But following the psalm to its glorious ending, an entirely new story begins to take shape:

And I will live for the LORD;
my descendants will serve you.

4. John Paul II, *Salvifici doloris*, 10.

The generation to come will be told of the Lord,
that they may proclaim to a people yet unborn
the deliverance you have brought. (Ps 22:31–32)

Whereas both sufferers and counselors may be speechless at the onset of suffering or grief, persevering through it with the Lord brings a wisdom and security that no other experience can teach. Others can tell you about it, encourage you through it, but only you can (and must) traverse the death-dark valley with the Lord, whom the Psalter evocatively identifies at this point as Shepherd:

The LORD is my shepherd, I shall not want;
he makes me lie down in green pastures.
He leads me beside still waters;
he restores my soul.
He leads me in paths of righteousness
for his name's sake.

Even though I walk through the valley of the
shadow of death,
I fear no evil;
for thou art with me;
thy rod and thy staff,
they comfort me.

Thou preparest a table before me
　　in the presence of my enemies;
thou anointest my head with oil,
　　my cup overflows.
Surely goodness and mercy shall follow me
　　all the days of my life;
and I shall dwell in the house of the LORD
　　for ever. (Ps 23)

What we need most in our grief isn't a neat, prepackaged answer. We need a Shepherd. We need a Savior to cling to. In our fears, we need a fearless One to guide us step-by-step. God does not want us to connect all the dots, not just yet. And that tells us something about how he wants our relationship with him to grow and develop.

Everyone knows that God brings good out of evil, that he allows evil for no other purpose. But we have to accept that his larger purpose in permitting evils is mostly hidden from us in this life. Acceptance does not come naturally as our first instinct, as St. John Paul II's beginning quote indicates. Nor does God demand an instant and perfect response from us. Saints from Abraham to Moses to the apostles to St. Teresa of Calcutta show us otherwise.

The Shepherd merely asks that we allow him to accompany us and show us the next step to take. He invites us into the most difficult and most meaningful dialog that human beings can ever have: the "Job" conversation, where affliction meets the Almighty, where our powerlessness kneels before the All-Powerful One, where our trust is stretched to its limits, and where finally we learn to pray.

Because it is in the asking, the listening, the silence, that God provides the ultimate answer for us in this life: peace in his will. Explanations only go so far. What God wants of us is trust. If we come away with only one point from reading the psalms of distress and anguish, it is that the speaker always returns to a sense of trust.

> In thee our fathers trusted;
>> they trusted, and thou didst deliver them.
> To thee they cried, and were saved;
>> in thee they trusted, and were not disappointed.
> (Ps 22:4–5)

God often allows humanly inexplicable sufferings in our lives as a part of the larger tapestry of his providence. We wouldn't mind losing everything if we knew that, in the end, all of the things that we had lost were being used to fashion something so beautiful that no human eye had ever seen, nor ear heard, nor human heart could ever have conceived. Yet it is in this light of faith that we have to see our own moments of darkness.

Sometimes God asks us to sacrifice something good and beautiful for the sake of drawing down a shower of graces and blessings for ourselves and others. Some of these sacrifices are chosen for us; others come by our own hand, even as the fallout of our own mistakes.

But tragedies or sufferings that have the potential to destroy a person's future can actually *open up* the future if handled with trust in God. Everyone can look back with regret on something irretrievably lost and say, "I wish I had it to do over again," or "I wish I could take that back," and so forth. Yet it is beyond our power to do so.

But it's not beyond God's power to bring some good out of it. I don't see how we can read the Gospels and come up with any other answer. I don't see how we can look at the lives of the saints and draw any other conclusion. We look at the Lord on the Cross and we see a broken and tortured man, doing what? Doing everything for us: loving us, saving us, encouraging us, embracing us, drawing all things to himself. And for those who are open to it, they are loved, encouraged, embraced, and saved.

The same Messiah who speaks words of dereliction at the beginning of Psalm 22 also bursts forth in praise of the God who listens and delivers him:

You who fear the LORD, praise him!
  all you sons of Jacob, glorify him,
  and stand in awe of him, all you sons of Israel!
For he has not despised or abhorred
  the affliction of the afflicted;
and he has not hid his face from him,
  but has heard, when he cried to him.

From thee comes my praise in the great
    congregation;
  my vows I will pay before those who fear him.
The afflicted shall eat and be satisfied;
  those who seek him shall praise the LORD!
  May your hearts live for ever! (Ps 22:23–26)

This is more than a textbook answer to the "problem of suffering." It is a coheir's sure and certain knowledge borne of perseverance, of hanging on the cross beside Jesus and finding him to be faithful, and a generous sharer of his glory.

In the end, suffering tends to produce one of two effects on people: it either draws them to God or drives them away from him. It can harden our hearts, break our hearts, depress us, or make us humble and receptive, where we say: "Speak, Lord, for your servant is *finally* listening" (cf. 1 Sm 3:9).

Bl. John Henry Newman cautions us about the two-edged sword that suffering often introduces into our lives. "We should never forget," he says,

> that trials and suffering by themselves have no power to make us holier or more heavenly. They make many men morose, selfish, and envious. The only sympathy they create in many minds, is the wish that others should suffer with them, not they with others. Affliction, when love is away, leads a man to wish others to be as he is; it leads to repining, malevolence, hatred, rejoicing in evil . . . Such is the effect of pain and sorrow, when unsanctified by God's saving grace.[5]

Seeing a purpose in suffering makes all the difference. We suffer with love and grace only when we see a purpose in it, a divine hand guiding us. Without that faith perspective, we could easily sink into the pitfalls Newman identifies: selfishness, hatred, resentment—even harboring a dark wish that others might endure our hardships—just so they will know what it's like to hurt as we do.

---

5. John Henry Newman, "Affliction, a School of Comfort," as quoted in *Parochial and Plain Sermons*, vol. 5, Sermon 25 (San Francisco: Ignatius Press, 1987), pp. 1139–1146.

If love "is not irritable or resentful;" if "it does not rejoice at wrong, but rejoices in the right;" if it "bears all things, believes all things, hopes all things, endures all things," then suffering without love opens us to all of the irritation, resentment, despair, and so forth, that love alone can fend off (cf. 1 Cor 13:4–7).

Only the Shepherd's love for us can make the difference between suffering that cripples and suffering that teaches us a new way to walk. The same breath in which the Scripture tells us to "walk in love," also points to the path trodden by the Suffering Shepherd in whose footsteps we must learn to walk: "Therefore be imitators of God, as beloved children. And walk in love, as Christ loved us and gave himself up for us, a fragrant offering and sacrifice to God" (Eph 5:1–2).

~~~~~

CHAPTER FIVE

Poor and Alone

Solitude and Loneliness

"The hour is coming, indeed it has come, when you will be scattered, every man to his home, and will leave me alone; yet I am not alone, for the Father is with me."

—JOHN 16:32

A priest friend once related to me the story of a young seminarian who had left the seminary because he felt lonely. He thought marriage, with its promise of close companionship, would stanch the emptiness he felt. Over time he did marry. But after a while he returned to the priest, disappointed. "When I was a seminarian," he told him, "I was one lonely man. Now that I am married, I am two lonely people."

His sad discovery takes nothing away from marriage as the close communion of life and love that it is. Rather, it reveals a common mistake discovered by single, celibate, and married alike: equating the absence of loneliness with the presence of others. The physical closeness of others, even of the most intimate kind, is no guarantee against the feeling of isolation. Some of the loneliest people in the world are those who are always "in a relationship" but who can never manage to connect on a deep level. In a culture of casual romantic relationships, everything hinges on an elusive (and illusionary) *chemistry*, which has more to do with animal instinct than the human need for communion of mind and heart.

In a sense, I could wish that the birth certificate of everyone born into this world, of whatever race or religion, should feature in indelible gold lettering the deservedly oft-quoted line from St. Augustine's *Confessions*: "You have made us for Yourself, O Lord, and our hearts are restless till they find rest in You."[1] This explains everything about our human loneliness and the solitude that, although bearing a striking resemblance, isn't at all the same thing.

The Psalms address both human loneliness and the solitude in which God is pursued and found. Not infrequently the Psalter dips into the darker regions of human isolation, from the quaint image of "a lonely

---

1. Augustine, *Confessions*, 1.1.

bird on the housetop" (Ps 102:7), to the dire confession: "My only friend is darkness" (Ps 88:19).[2] But there are times when both rooftop and darkness are chosen in response to grace, and become the privileged venue of encounter with the living God. And this is solitude. The Lord sometimes wants to get us alone—far from the "props" of daily life, from the normal run of events and pressures—to draw out sentiments that can only come from a posture of complete dependence and poverty.

> Incline thy ear, O Lord, and answer me,
> > for I am poor and needy. (Ps 86:1)

> For God alone my soul waits in silence,
> > from him comes my salvation.
> He only is my rock and my salvation,
> > my fortress; I shall not be greatly moved.

> For God alone my soul waits in silence,
> > for my hope is from him.
> He only is my rock and my salvation,
> > my fortress; I shall not be shaken. (Ps 62:1–2, 5–6)

We humans have an ambivalent relationship with being alone—we might even add, an ambivalent

---

2. Confraternity Version.

relationship with *ourselves*. St. Augustine, once again, hits the mark when he says, "I am a burden to myself, as not being full of You."[3] Being alone both attracts and repels for the same reason: what we find there defines the quality of the aloneness. If I find only self, I will find only the limitations and frustrations that need redemption. Whereas I need to find the Redeemer. I, the self-burdening individual, need to rest myself in the shadow of him who invites me to unburden myself *of* self and to take upon my shoulders his yoke, the burden of which is easy and light.[4]

Here a helpful distinction is in order. Loneliness, unlike solitude, is the painful awareness not only of being *alone* but of being cut-off from others— "unfriended" and unable to connect. "I looked for pity, but there was none," the psalm says plaintively, "and for comforters, but I found none" (Ps 69:20).

Loneliness can be felt in ways both deeply spiritual and deeply human. Sometimes it is self-induced, as we will see below. But it need not be a fault to feel it,

---

3. Augustine, *Confessions*, 10. 28.39. The entire passage reads: "When I shall cleave unto Thee with all my being, then shall I in nothing have pain and labour; and my life shall be a real life, being wholly full of Thee. But now since he whom Thou fillest is the one Thou liftest up, I am a burden to myself, as not being full of Thee."

4. Cf. Mt 11:28–30. Also worth reading is St. Augustine's reference to these verses in *Confessions*, 9.1.

as the example of the saints shows. St. Teresa of Avila mentions a number of times how the absence of a good friend or spiritual guide—no less than the likes of St. John of the Cross and Fr. Jerome Gracián—pains her with loneliness.

> [T]he next day I became sorely afflicted in seeing I was without him [Gracián], since I had no one to whom I could have recourse in this tribulation. It seemed to me I was living in great loneliness, and this loneliness increased when I saw that there was no one now but him who might give me comfort and that he had to be absent most of the time, which was a great torment to me.[5]

Or with good humor to a fellow nun:

> I was amused, daughter, at how groundless is your complaining, for you have in your very midst *mi padre* Fray John of the Cross, a heavenly and divine man. I tell you, daughter, from the time he left and went down there I have not found anyone in all Castile like him, or anyone who communicates so much fervor for walking along the way to heaven. You will not believe the feeling of loneliness that

---

5. Teresa of Avila, *Spiritual Testimonies*: 53, in *The Collected Works of St. Teresa of Avila*, p. 415.

his absence causes me. Realize what a great treasure you have there in that saint.[6]

Loneliness as the painful awareness of isolation transcends both place and circumstances. A busy street, the middle of a crowd, even the company of family and friends, can supply the setting for feeling cut off from others. Because, again, the problem is not mainly with other people, or with one's environment, but with (and within) oneself.

Where loneliness becomes a fault, a personal problem, is in having a disordered desire for love and companionship that no one can reasonably or realistically fulfill. St. John Paul addressed the problem of loneliness among priests in words that could be applied to everyone:

There is a loneliness which all priests experience and which is completely normal. But there is another loneliness which is the product of various difficulties and which in turn creates further difficulties.[7]

---

6. Teresa of Avila, *The Collected Letters of St. Teresa of Avila*, vol. 2, trans. Kieran Kavanaugh (Washington, D.C.: ICS, 2001), pp. 145–146.

7. John Paul II, Post-Synodal Apostolic Exhortation *Pastores dabo vobis* (March 15, 1992), 74.

Without oversimplifying the "difficulties" involved here, many of which can be beyond one's control, Ven. Fulton J. Sheen identifies the causes of loneliness that lie at the root of most of the difficulties:

> The basic cause of loneliness is the excessive desire to be loved, for this creates an atmosphere of love-lessness. The more we seek to be loved, the less we are loved. The less we are loved, the less lovable we become. And the less lovable we become, the less capable we become of loving anyone else.[8]

Loneliness is not really a matter of being by yourself when you would rather be with others. It is more an attitude of neediness where one makes emotional demands on others that they can seldom live up to. It is equivalent to creating an emotional bottomless pit that no one's attention or interest will ever be able to fill.

When Archbishop Sheen speaks of an "excessive desire to be loved," he does not mean that we should not desire love; in fact, we cannot help desiring to love and to be loved. And that's a good thing, a God-given thing. But as often happens in fallen creatures, we seek good things in a *disordered* way. Seeking human love in a disordered way ultimately means wanting others to

---

8. Fulton J. Sheen, *Footprints in a Darkened Forest* (New York: Meredith Press, 1967), p. 25.

love us in a way that only God can: perfectly, unfailingly, with complete understanding of all our needs. Not even the best of friends, of spouses, can meet that expectation.

It should be added that most of the time people who think and act in this disordered fashion are simply unaware of it. It is too much a part of who they are for them to have the distance, the perspective, to step back and evaluate it. All they may be able to identify within themselves is a vague but powerful craving for attention coupled with an equally vague hope that someone, someday, will eventually come to save them. When this fails to happen, something has to fill the gap created by disappointed expectations.

Any number of self-destructive escapes are chosen as a desperate attempt to fill the void created by feeling isolated: intoxication, sexual acting-out, physically harming oneself, not excluding suicide. Each person handles loneliness in his own way, either virtuously or not. And since it is hard to handle any kind of pain, physical or emotional, *virtuously*, it is clear that many of the sins and addictions people fall into are a result of how they choose to handle the pain of loneliness.

We have to avoid creating unreasonable expectations of others for approval, affirmation, and support. We should offer these important things to others; charity is expressed very powerfully through them. But we can never expect anyone to be "God" to us: to love us out of our misery. This love can only come from the inside, a love that he brings by his presence within us. How beautiful it is to be an instrument of God's grace and healing! But only God is the Healer.

Whatever the cause of loneliness, the Psalms reveal the sacred author quite unselfconsciously giving vent to his distress. And this tells us not only that it is an unavoidable experience, but that it must have a spiritual value in God's eyes that we don't want to disregard. We can actually grow from it.

The fact is, many people find their way to God by first passing through human loneliness, even of the "culpable" kind, the type created by unreasonable expectations. If we are open to grace, God will use any crevice in the soul to get in, whether it's an open door or a broken-out window. Few have better described this gateway of human perplexity and desolation than Bl. John Henry Newman. In a meditation especially treasured by St. Teresa of Calcutta,[9] Newman movingly pleads his case before Jesus in psalm-like fashion, crafting a prayer every lonely person should tuck into his or her prayer book:

---

9. Mother Teresa prescribed that a portion of this meditation be recited by her Missionary of Charity Sisters each day after Holy Communion.

Thou . . . art the only Light of my soul.

Thou enlightenest every man that cometh into
   this world.

I am utterly dark, as dark as hell, without
   Thee. . . .

Thou comest and goest at Thy will. O my God,
   I cannot keep Thee!

I can only beg of Thee to stay.

"*Mane nobiscum, Domine, quoniam advesperascit.*"[10]

Remain till morning, and then go not without
   giving me a blessing.

Remain with me till death in this dark valley,
   when the darkness will end.

Remain, O Light of my soul, *iam advesperascit!*

The gloom, which is not Thine, falls over me.

I am nothing. I have little command of myself.
   I cannot do what I would.

I am disconsolate and sad. I want something,
   I know not what.

It is Thou that I want, though I so little understand this.

I say it and take it on faith; I partially understand
   it, but very poorly.

---

10. Cf. Lk 24:29: "Stay with us, for it is toward evening and the
day is now far spent."

Shine on me, *O Ignis semper ardens et nunquam deficiens!*—

"O fire ever burning and never failing"—

and I shall begin, through and in Thy Light, to see Light,

and to recognise Thee truly, as the Source of Light.

Mane nobiscum; stay, sweet Jesus, stay for ever.

In this decay of nature, give more grace.

Stay with me, and then I shall begin to shine as Thou shinest:

so to shine as to be a light to others.

The light, O Jesus, will be all from Thee. None of it will be mine.

No merit to me. It will be Thou who shinest through me upon others.

O let me thus praise Thee, in the way which Thou dost love best,

by shining on all those around me.

Give light to them as well as to me; light them with me, through me. Teach me to show forth Thy praise, Thy truth, Thy will.

Make me preach Thee without preaching—

not by words, but by my example and by the catching force,

the sympathetic influence, of what I do—
by my visible resemblance to Thy saints,
and the evident fulness of the love which my heart
    bears to Thee.[11]

Sometimes solitude must first pass by way of loneliness. They may feel alike and look alike, but eventually loneliness shows itself to be utterly barren—not the soil where intimate union with God grows. As Newman eloquently shows us here, the real breakthrough comes when loneliness forces the soul to a kind of crisis: the decision must be made to fold in on self or turn outward to God and neighbor. The painstaking inner journey charted by Newman erupts in a cry to God, a cry made in faith. It calls upon the Lord to do for us what he promises to do for all mankind: *Draw us to himself and be with us always*—music to the ears of the lonely.

Loneliness is a special suffering, a record of tears and restlessness (cf. Ps 56) which is explored in agonizing depth by the Psalms. But it remains a largely negative and self-defeating experience, as long as it remains a dead end. "Like a bird caught in a net," says

---

11. John Henry Newman, "Jesus, the Light of the Soul," as quoted in *Prayers, Verses and Devotions* (San Francisco: Ignatius Press, 2000), pp. 389–90.

Archbishop Sheen on loneliness, "we deepen our tragedy."[12] Any painful experience that fails to lead us to
God is ultimately a dead end.

Solitude is also a special kind of agony, but wholly
different in orientation. Here, we are turned toward
the Lord, waiting on him, hoping in him, pleading
with him for closer and deeper communion.

The Psalms tell us of a deep, heartfelt yearning for
the Lord that exceeds all of our other longings; it is not
only healthy, but even a great sign of spiritual progress.
This is what saints and mystics call *solitude*. In the language of the Bible it comes across as hunger and thirst,
as restlessness for the Lord.

> As a hart longs
> > for flowing streams,
> so longs my soul
> > for thee, O God.
> My soul thirsts for God,
> > for the living God.
> When shall I come and behold
> > the face of God?
> My tears have been my food
> > day and night,

---

12. Sheen, *Footprints*, p. 25.

while men say to me continually,
  "Where is your God?"

These things I remember,
  as I pour out my soul:
how I went with the throng,
  and led them in procession to the house of God,
with glad shouts and songs of thanksgiving,
  a multitude keeping festival.
Why are you cast down, O my soul,
  and why are you disquieted within me?
Hope in God; for I shall again praise him,
  my help and my God. (Ps 42:1–6)

The psalmist's nostalgia for the Lord, his longing for the courts of the Temple, preoccupies him day and night. This singleness of desire creates the solitude he carries about within himself. Unlike an appetite that ceases craving once it's been satisfied, the desire for God cannot be stilled simply by feeding on food or drinking a drink or by distracting entertainments. God is infinite. Every contact we have with him, even (and especially) in Holy Communion, increases our hunger for him.

"Come to me, you who desire me,
and eat your fill of my produce.

For the remembrance of me is sweeter than honey,
   and my inheritance sweeter than the
      honeycomb.
Those who eat me will hunger for more,
   and those who drink me will thirst for more."
  (Sir 24:19–21)

The man who hungers and thirsts merely for food or drink is not a solitary. He is a survivor only. The one who hungers and thirsts for God feels alone and, in a healthy sense, disconnected from the world around him. He knows he cannot survive without him.

Whom have I in heaven but thee?
   And there is nothing upon earth that I desire
      besides thee.
My flesh and my heart may fail,
   but God is the strength of my heart and my
      portion for ever.

For lo, those who are far from thee shall perish;
   thou dost put an end to those who are false
      to thee.
But for me it is good to be near God;
   I have made the Lord God my refuge,
   that I may tell of all thy works. (Ps 73:25–28)

Solitude is bittersweet; the Psalms and the saints consider it as both an agony and an ecstasy. Witness St. Teresa of Jesus:

> I often reflect, my Lord, that if there is something by which life can endure being separated from You, it is solitude. For the soul rests in the quiet of solitude; yet, since it is not completely free for the enjoyment of solitude, the torment is often doubled.[13]

If the Psalms give us to understand that loneliness waits upon God because the soul feels abandoned and forgotten, then solitude waits in silence for the Lord because he has already given her a pledge, a foretaste, of how delightful his presence is: "O taste and see that the LORD is good!" (Ps 34:8). Solitude creates and heightens hunger for the Lord. It is an acquired taste, but one the Lord freely gives to those who seek him: "The young lions suffer want and hunger; but those who seek the LORD lack no good thing" (Ps 34:10).

St. John of the Cross compares our appetites to caverns whose capacity for God deepens as lesser things cease to satisfy them:

---

13. Teresa of Avila, *Soliloquies*, 2, in *The Collected Works of St. Teresa of Avila*, p. 443.

The capacity of these caverns is deep because the object of this capacity, namely God, is profound and infinite. Thus in a certain fashion their capacity is infinite, their thirst is infinite, their hunger is also deep and infinite, and their languishing and suffering are infinite death. Although the suffering is not as intense as is the suffering of the next life, yet the soul is a living image of that infinite privation, since it is in a certain way disposed to receive its plenitude. This suffering, however, is of another quality because it lies within the recesses of the will's love; and love is not what alleviates the pain, since the greater the love, so much more impatient are such persons for the possession of God, for whom they hope at times with intense longing.[14]

The same saint of Carmel also equates solitude with the poverty of spirit of the first Beatitude, as well as with the renunciation of all things on which the Lord conditions discipleship: "Whoever of you does not renounce all that he has cannot be my disciple" (Lk 14:33).[15]

---

14. John of the Cross, *The Living Flame of Love*: 3.22, in *The Collected Works of Saint John of the Cross*, trans. Kieran Kavanaugh and Otilio Rodriguez, rev. ed. (Washington, D.C.: ICS, 1991), pp. 681–2.

15. John of the Cross, *The Living Flame of Love*: 3.46, pp. 691–2.

Being alone for the right reasons demands spiritual maturity. And spiritual maturity is acquired by our willingness to remain alone and poor, detached and hopeful, for the right reasons. Jesus deliberately went off to pray alone, and even invited the apostles to "Come away by yourselves to a lonely place, and rest a while" (Mk 6:31). Then we should hear this as a call to deeper communion with the Lord, even if we don't quite know where we're going or what to do with ourselves when we're apart from others. The purpose of solitude is not to be left alone with no one to bother us. It is rather to ready us to wait upon God, whether we're physically alone or not. It is not to wait upon an experience, much less an ecstasy, but wherever we are to be ever seeking the Lord as our heart's desire: his will, his grace, his consolation.

A story from the life of St. Josemaría Escrivá illustrates this very concretely. The context of the episode is especially significant. While serving as chaplain to Augustinian nuns in Madrid in the early 1930s, he found himself one day unable to make a recollected, focused thanksgiving after morning Mass: "I wanted to pray after Mass, in the quiet of the church. I didn't succeed."[16]

---

16. Josemaría Escrivá, *Intimate Notes*, no. 334, as quoted in Andrés Vázquez de Prada, *The Founder of Opus Dei*, vol. 1 (New York: Scepter, 2001), p. 333.

Feeling uncharacteristically restless, he left the church, bought a newspaper, and boarded a streetcar—and that's when God touched him. In the saint's own words:

> I felt the action of the Lord. He was making spring forth in my heart and on my lips, with the force of something imperatively necessary, this tender invocation: *Abba! Pater!* I was out on the street, in a streetcar. . . . Probably I made that prayer out loud.
>
> And I walked the streets of Madrid for maybe an hour, maybe two, I can't say; time passed without my being aware of it. They must have thought I was crazy. I was contemplating, with lights that were not mine, that amazing truth. It was like a lighted coal burning in my soul, never to be extinguished.[17]

This episode gives a more than theoretical expression to the meaning of solitude. God does not involve himself in our lives by remote control. He is present to the soul; he is the life of the soul, in the deepest possible way. So that the quality of our relationship with him is not completely dependent on our

---

17. Josemaría Escrivá, *Apuntes*, no. 60, and *Letter 8 Dec 1949*, no. 41, as quoted in Vázquez de Prada, p. 334.

circumstances, but on our openness to the grace of his presence wherever we are. St. Josemaría often taught this message as the root spirituality not only of Opus Dei but of the Christian life itself: You can be "a good child of God" wherever you are and through whatever occupation you undertake. But you can only be that child of God by nurturing an interior awareness of the gift of your adoption.

The contemplation and conviction St. Josemaría experienced in the streets and streetcars of a Madrid morning is given a poetic turn by Hubert van Zeller. Expressing the same reality of discovering Christ in the unique (even *urban*) solitudes of daily life, he writes:

> Saints are not those who have won their way to the topmost pinnacles: they are those who have lost their way in the backstreets, following after Christ whom they are always just missing. But they have not in fact missed Him, for He lost all and they bear their loss with Him.[18]

This is in line with one of the Bible's most vehement expressions of love. The bride of the Song of Solomon is painfully aware of her loneliness, but refuses to sulk in her bedchamber. Instead she races

---

18. Hubert van Zeller, OSB, *The Choice of God* (London: Burns & Oats, 1956; reprinted 1963), p. 123.

into the city at night, traversing its streets and squares
with the one-track mind of a holy solitary:

> Upon my bed by night
>> I sought him whom my soul loves;
> I sought him, but found him not;
>> I called him, but he gave no answer.
> "I will rise now and go about the city,
>> in the streets and in the squares;
> I will seek him whom my soul loves."
>> I sought him, but found him not.
> The watchmen found me,
>> as they went about in the city.
> "Have you seen him whom my soul loves?"
> Scarcely had I passed them,
>> when I found him whom my soul loves.
> I held him, and would not let him go. . . .
>> (SONG 3:1–4)

If St. Josemaría, and plenty of other saints, could
find God in morning commuter traffic, on bustling
sidewalks—or in the case of saints like Maximilian
Kolbe, in a concentration camp—then solitude is
clearly not the exclusive province of hermits, monks,
or nuns. Of course, by vocation they take radical
means to create an environment where this aloneness

with God can happen more readily—austerity of life, simplicity of meals and furnishings, etc. But the Lord does not abandon the vast majority of Christians also called by baptism to a deep one-on-one relationship with him. This is the promise of Jesus:

> I will not leave you desolate; I will come to you. Yet a little while, and the world will see me no more, but you will see me; because I live, you will live also. In that day you will know that I am in my Father, and you in me, and I in you. He who has my commandments and keeps them, he it is who loves me; and he who loves me will be loved by my Father, and I will love him and manifest myself to him." Judas (not Iscariot) said to him, "Lord, how is it that you will manifest yourself to us, and not to the world?" Jesus answered him, "If a man loves me, he will keep my word, and my Father will love him, and we will come to him and make our home with him. (Jn 14:18–23)

Some lessons are not only best taught by experience, but *only* taught by experience. We can't simply read about solitude and human loneliness and "get" how or why they should lead us to God. Sometimes the Lord will allow us to feel "desolate" or lonely to motivate us to seek him to exercise our heartfelt desire for him.

The Psalms overflow with prayerful, urgent cries from one who isn't merely imagining what it feels like to be abandoned. A man in agony speaks:

Hear my prayer, O LORD;
  let my cry come to thee!
Do not hide thy face from me
  in the day of my distress!
Incline thy ear to me;
  answer me speedily in the day when I call!
  (Ps 102:1–2)

Rouse thyself! Why sleepest thou, O Lord?
  Awake! Do not cast us off forever!
Why dost thou hide thy face?
  Why dost thou forget our affliction and
    oppression?
For our soul is bowed down to the dust;
  our body cleaves to the ground.
Rise up, come to our help!
  Deliver us for the sake of thy steadfast love!
  (Ps 44:23–26)

It is time for the LORD to act. (Ps 119:126)

Is there anyone who likes to feel this way, inadequate, humbled, poor and needy? No one.

Unless, that is, we can see our utter poverty and loneliness as God's way of preparing us for light, love, and deeper friendship. This is not a kind of game he plays with us. There is really no other way for us to lay hold of closeness with God unless we are more than "theoretically" convinced that poverty of spirit and total lack of reliance on ourselves really do lead us to God.

It is the parched earth that is most receptive to moisture, the hungry who best appreciate food, the uninhabited land that most marvelously displays the fruitful growth that only the Lord can bring about.

> He turns a desert into pools of water,
>> a parched land into springs of water.
> And there he lets the hungry dwell,
>> and they establish a city to live in;
> they sow fields, and plant vineyards,
>> and get a fruitful yield. . . .
> Whoever is wise, let him give heed to these
>> things;
>> let men consider the steadfast love of the LORD.
>> (Ps 107:35–37, 43)

The Lord's "steadfast love" must be our anchor—the anchor that keeps us firm and unwavering as we wait on him.

Whether we wait in solitude or languish in loneliness, a perfect psalm to have on our lips is one that
reminds us just how close the Lord is to us, just how
thoroughly we are seen and known by him:

> O Lord, thou hast searched me and known me!
>> Thou knowest when I sit down and when I rise up;
>> thou discernest my thoughts from afar.
> Thou searchest out my path and my lying down,
>> and art acquainted with all my ways.
> Even before a word is on my tongue,
>> lo, O Lord, thou knowest it altogether.
> Thou dost beset me behind and before,
>> and layest thy hand upon me.
> Such knowledge is too wonderful for me;
>> it is high, I cannot attain it.
>
> Whither shall I go from thy Spirit?
>> Or whither shall I flee from thy presence?
> If I ascend to heaven, thou art there!
>> If I make my bed in Sheol, thou art there!
> If I take the wings of the morning
>> and dwell in the uttermost parts of the sea,
> even there thy hand shall lead me,
>> and thy right hand shall hold me.

If I say, "Let only darkness cover me,
   and the light about me be night,"
even the darkness is not dark to thee,
   the night is bright as the day;
   for darkness is as light with thee.

For thou didst form my inward parts,
   thou didst knit me together in my mother's
      womb.
I praise thee, for thou art fearful and wonderful.
   Wonderful are thy works!
Thou knowest me right well;
   my frame was not hidden from thee,
when I was being made in secret,
   intricately wrought in the depths of the earth.
Thy eyes beheld my unformed substance;
   in thy book were written, every one of them,
the days that were formed for me,
   when as yet there was none of them.
How precious to me are thy thoughts, O God!
   How vast is the sum of them!
If I would count them, they are more than
   the sand.
   When I awake, I am still with thee. (Ps 139:1–18)

~ↄ

A New Song, a New Life, a New Love

A song is a thing of joy; more profoundly, it is a thing of love. Anyone, therefore, who has learned to love the new life has learned to sing a new song, and the new song reminds us of our new life.

—ST. AUGUSTINE[1]

God relies on any number of created things to get our attention. And the surest way to our hearts and minds is through our senses. Catholics are especially acclimated to the sights, sounds, and fragrances native to their solemn liturgy: vestment colors and textures, precious metals, incense, and sacred music each move a bodily sense upward to the Lord. What St. John Paul II once said about Gregorian chant, designating it as "the music of the Church's faith," is true of all sacred art: "[t]he 'beautiful' [is] thus wedded to the 'true,' so that through art too souls

---

1. Augustine, Commentary on Psalm 149, Sermon 34.

might be lifted up from the world of the senses to the eternal."[2] There is a transparency, a clarity, in beauty that leads to God:

> One thing have I asked of the Lord, that will
>   I seek after;
> that I may dwell in the house of the Lord
>   all the days of my life,
> to behold the beauty of the Lord,
>   and to inquire in his temple. (Ps 27:4)

> Honor and majesty are before him;
>   strength and beauty are in his sanctuary.
>   (Ps 96:6)

St. Augustine testifies to the power of beauty in the liturgical setting of cathedral worship. Years after his baptism at the hands of St. Ambrose in Milan, he fondly recalled the chants of Ambrose's cathedral: "How greatly did I weep in Your hymns and canticles, deeply moved by the voices of Your sweet-speaking Church!"[3] And these, undoubtedly, were comprised mainly of psalms.

But beyond the walls of a church building, whatever will penetrate our thick heads and hard hearts is

---

2. John Paul II, *Letter to Artists* (April 4, 1999), *www.vatican.va.*

3. Augustine, *Confessions*, 9.6.

fair game in God's hands. Both the beautiful and the fearful can lead us to him. Thus he created a beautiful world that enchants, but which in its fallen state also frightens by its unpredictable and devastating energy. Scripture testifies as much to the power of storms and earthquakes to convert, as to the sublimity of the created order to advertise God's glory.

To some he gives the talent for art. Used rightly it leads people to truth, and thus closer to God who is *the* Truth. Music, sacred music in particular, is one of these divine guides, drawing the soul upward to the eternal, as St. John Paul II points out. His successor on the throne of Peter, Pope Benedict XVI, finds in "musical expression" a more fully human response to God:

> . . . musical expression is part of the proper human response to God's self-revelation, to his becoming open to a relationship with us. Mere speech, mere silence, mere action are not enough. The integral way of humanly expressing joy or sorrow, consent or complaint which occurs in singing is necessary for responding to God, who touches us precisely in the totality of our being.[4]

---

4. Joseph Ratzinger (Benedict XVI), *A New Song for the Lord: Faith in Christ and Liturgy Today*, trans. Martha M. Matesich (New York: Crossroad Publishing, 1996), p. 126.

Sacred music, then, is more than a sort of holy background music to prayer, something to enjoy passively.
It is also an instrument of worship which the Lord,
especially through the Psalms, places on our lips, and
in our hands, to use.

> Praise the LORD with the lyre,
>> make melody to him with the harp of ten strings!
> Sing to him a new song,
>> play skilfully on the strings, with loud shouts.
>> (Ps 33:2–3)

> O come, let us sing to the LORD;
>> let us make a joyful noise to the rock of our
>>> salvation!
> Let us come into his presence with thanksgiving;
>> let us make a joyful noise to him with songs
>>> of praise! (Ps 95:1–2)

Even shouting and clapping are sanctioned ways of
worship: "Clap your hands, all peoples! Shout to God
with loud songs of joy!" (47:1).

If theme songs, background music, commercial
jingles, and movie soundtracks are any indication, people like to live their lives to musical accompaniment.
For many, music serves not only to accentuate but also
to interpret significant life moments. The fact that pop

music charts register like seismographs from week to week indicates that although 'favorites' change, the human desire to live accompanied by song does not.

"Music has charms to soothe the savage breast,"[5] William Congreve famously wrote, testifying to music's power to accomplish more than delighting the ear. It pacifies, excites, and, among other of its powers, reawakens memories even of things long past. Perhaps even more than fragrance or touch or a souvenir, nothing so ties us to an experience as music. A poignant song heard when falling in love, or at a moment of great celebration or sorrow, can stay with us a lifetime, vividly reviving the moment whenever we hear it.

Although people sometimes listen to music for reasons largely practical, like staying alert while driving or sustaining the momentum of an exercise routine, a closer look may also reveal important information about our psychological, emotional, and affective lives. Anything we love passionately, or dislike vehemently, cannot help but reveal our values and character. Augustine's tears are clearly not those of someone merely charmed by stirring melodies, but of a man overwhelmed by the mercies of God.

---

5. Often misquoted as "Music has charms to soothe the savage beast," the line comes from Congreve's play *The Mourning Bride* (1697).

If our individual life experiences resonate in music, what can we say about the single most important event in the life of the world? If at the coming of Christ time restarted, and if the Paschal Mystery marks the passage from death to life for all reborn in him, then shouldn't the redeemed have a unique music all their own—timeless and renewing—to go along with it?

Our Redemption has a song. The Psalms call it, simply, the *new song*. A song that celebrates an event, a Redeemer, that never ages and always sounds fresh, is always relevant and never outdated, that is the new song. St. Augustine's golden phrase "ever ancient, ever new" applies as much to the eternal and unchanging Lord as to the saving events wrought by the Lord for our salvation, and it is of these that the new song sings.[6]

What makes it new and timeless isn't a continual change of melody or of words. It's not the song that changes, but the singers of it. The song continues to express the same kinds of things. But as we experience the continuing renewal, and reforms, of Christian life, the song gathers a deeper meaning. Like a great work of literature whose layers of meaning only reveal themselves over many readings, our appreciation for what God has done for us and continues to do in our lives deepens over time.

---

6. Augustine, *Confessions*, 10.27.

Pope Benedict XVI comments that the Psalms' "ever-recurring imperative" to sing a new song to the Lord stems from this ongoing reality of salvation—not accomplished once-for-all: "Experiences of salvation are found not only in the past, but occur over and over again; hence they also require the ever-new proclamation of God's contemporaneity."[7] God is close at hand in our present struggle, whatever that might entail. Jesus is still our Savior, because although his work of redemption is an accomplished event, salvation is ongoing.

When St. Paul tells us to "work out your own salvation with fear and trembling" (Phil 2:12), he means a continuing, daily struggle against the world, the flesh, and the devil, which is very real. Victories and losses are quite concrete—enough to elate, depress, or discourage. This conflict demands the singing of the new song, a song of thanksgiving and praise, for today's salvation:

> I waited patiently for the LORD;
>> he inclined to me and heard my cry.
> He drew me up from the desolate pit,
>> out of the miry bog,

---

7. Benedict XVI, *A New Song for the Lord*, p. 127.

and set my feet upon a rock,
> making my steps secure.
He put a new song in my mouth,
> a song of praise to our God. (Ps 40:1–3)

The Lord never wants us to forget our moments of salvation, especially the monumental ones. Times of deep conversion, occasions when death seemed imminent but was unexpectedly averted, a debilitating temptation overcome—these are the real milestones of our lives in Christ. No less deserving of the new song is repentance and reconciliation in the wake of moral failure, of sins committed. Sin, in itself, is never a cause for rejoicing. It is, rather, the goodness and mercy of God which our failings occasion. This is what the new song celebrates.

And it is for this reason that the Church's Easter liturgy dares to declare the original sin of Adam a *felix culpa* (a happy fault), since it occasioned the universal redemption wrought by Jesus Christ, "so great, so glorious a Redeemer."[8] Significantly, this phrase comes from the first solemn chant of the Easter Vigil,

---

8. "The Easter Proclamation (*Exsultet*)" in *The Roman Missal*, trans. The International Commission on English in the Liturgy, 3rd typical ed. (Washington, D.C.: United States Catholic Conference of Bishops, 2011), 19.

the "Exsultet," setting the tone for the entire liturgy, whose readings and psalms survey both the creative and saving actions of God from the world's creation to its spiritual recreation in Christ.

As the several readings unfold, and the interspersed psalms provide songful responses to God's mighty works, we are never to bypass the inspired lens through which the Church has us view the events of salvation history: "O happy fault that earned so great, so glorious a Redeemer!" Had the Church not said it first, we might hold our tongues. But it's a truth that demands proclamation in the grandest language we can find: God is greater than sin. Joy in the saving Lord incredibly outweighs the sad gravity of human offenses. The only appropriate human response is to sing our thanksgiving and praise in the wake of this completely gratuitous mercy.

From ancient times, the Easter liturgy of the Church has done just this in featuring Psalm 118. Its verses urge praise, thanksgiving, and "glad songs of victory" for the day of salvation whose architect could only be the Lord:

> Out of my distress I called on the LORD;
>   the LORD answered me and set me free.
> With the LORD on my side I do not fear.
>   What can man do to me?

I was pushed hard, so that I was falling,
    but the LORD helped me.
The LORD is my strength and my song;
    he has become my salvation.

Hark, glad songs of victory
    in the tents of the righteous:
"The right hand of the LORD does valiantly,
    the right hand of the LORD is exalted,
    the right hand of the LORD does valiantly!"
I shall not die, but I shall live,
    and recount the deeds of the LORD.

I thank thee that thou hast answered me
    and hast become my salvation.
The stone which the builders rejected
    has become the head of the corner.
This is the LORD's doing;
    it is marvelous in our eyes.
This is the day which the LORD has made;
    let us rejoice and be glad in it.
    (Ps 118:5–6, 13–17, 21–24)

God's wisdom has inspired singing to punctuate some of the most epochal moments in salvation history, and this should teach us something about our

own path of salvation. The central saving event of the
Old Covenant, Israel's exodus from Egypt, with its
divinely-engineered defeat of Pharaoh and his army, was
celebrated musically on the far shore of the Red Sea:

> Then Moses and the people of Israel sang this song
> to the LORD, saying,

> "I will sing to the LORD, for he has triumphed
>   gloriously;
>   the horse and his rider he has thrown into
>   the sea.
> The LORD is my strength and my song,
>   and he has become my salvation;
> this is my God, and I will praise him." (Ex 15:1–2)

> Then Miriam, the prophetess, the sister of Aaron,
> took a timbrel in her hand; and all the women
> went out after her with timbrels and dancing. And
> Miriam sang to them:

> "Sing to the LORD, for he has triumphed
>   gloriously;
>   the horse and his rider he has thrown into
>   the sea." (Ex 15:20–21)

The Norbertine Order celebrates a unique liturgical rite of vespers (evening prayer) during Easter season

that ritually recreates this most monumental saving event in the Old Testament. Called *Paschal Vespers*, it features a procession to the baptismal font of the abbey church, while the confreres sing—often from memory, always in Latin chant—the verses of Psalm 114.

When Israel went forth from Egypt,
    the house of Jacob from a people of strange
        language,
Judah became his sanctuary,
    Israel his dominion.

The sea looked and fled,
    Jordan turned back.
The mountains skipped like rams,
    the hills like lambs.

What ails you, O sea, that you flee?
    O Jordan, that you turn back?
O mountains, that you skip like rams?
    O hills, like lambs?

Tremble, O earth, at the presence of the LORD,
    at the presence of the God of Jacob,
who turns the rock into a pool of water,
    the flint into a spring of water.

Having reached the font, the priest presiding over the Paschal Vespers then performs the "asperges" or the sprinkling of the assembled confreres with holy water, passing through their midst as he does so, as through a symbolic Red Sea: "He divided the sea and let them pass through it, and made the waters stand like a heap" (Ps 78:13).

Reenacting in symbol and sacrament the events of our salvation, accompanied by the sacred chanting of the new song, beautifully renews our kinship with the redeemed of every time and place. Those who first followed the Savior through the Red Sea are elders and ancestors to us who pass, not only through the aisles of a church, but through the streets and corridors of the modern world, following in spirit and truth the Paschal Lamb who was slain for us. Conditions change, cultures come and go, but the salvation of which we sing goes on.

At the dawn of the New Testament, we find another Miriam, the central figure in the Incarnation of the new Moses, chanting her own hymn of praise. Coming directly out of the rich Hebrew heritage of Psalms, hymns, and spiritual canticles, the Blessed Virgin spontaneously composes a canticle in keeping with her own prayer tradition and significantly contributing to it:

And Mary said,

"My soul magnifies the Lord,
and my spirit rejoices in God my Savior,
for he has regarded the low estate of his
     handmaiden.
For behold, henceforth all generations will call
     me blessed;
for he who is mighty has done great things for me,
and holy is his name.
And his mercy is on those who fear him
from generation to generation.
He has shown strength with his arm,
he has scattered the proud in the imagination
     of their hearts,
he has put down the mighty from their thrones,
and exalted those of low degree;
he has filled the hungry with good things,
and the rich he has sent empty away.
He has helped his servant Israel,
in remembrance of his mercy,
as he spoke to our fathers,
to Abraham and to his posterity for ever."
     (Lk 1:46–55)

I quote in full an already familiar text to illustrate how one immersed in her own tradition naturally fashions prayer from pre-existing models while personalizing the message. In this new song, Mary responds not only to a new moment of salvation, but to Salvation itself, the salvation made flesh in her womb, the Son whose name means *Salvation*.

We saw this kind of prayer-weaving earlier in St. Gregory of Narek, as he composed a "new book of Psalms." Woven from threads both ancient and new, yet plaited together seamlessly, they amount to a collection of *new songs*. The universal appeal of the Psalter causes St. Gregory to comment in words directly applicable to our Lady: "The Psalms were songs of everything for the pure in heart: a testament of life, written for all people."[9]

Not long after Mary's Magnificat, an outpouring of angelic praise surrounds the Lord's birth:

> And suddenly there was with the angel a multitude of the heavenly host praising God and saying, "Glory to God in the highest, and on earth peace among men with whom he is pleased!" (Lk 2:13–14)

St. John Chrysostom elaborates on this musical scene. In a famous Christmas sermon he explains

---

9. Narek, *Speaking with God*, Prayer 51 C.

the yearning to share in the canticle and dance of the angels and shepherds:

> Since therefore all rejoice, I too desire to rejoice. I too wish to share the choral dance, to celebrate the festival. But I take my part, not plucking the harp, not shaking the Thyrsian staff, not with the music of the pipes, nor holding a torch, but holding in my arms the cradle of Christ. For this is all my hope, this my life, this my salvation, this my pipe, my harp. And bearing it I come, and having from its power received the gift of speech, I too, with the angels, sing: *Glory to God in the Highest;* and with the shepherds, *and on earth peace to men of good will.*[10]

On the night of the Last Supper, our Lord and the apostles also sang: "And when they had sung a hymn, they went out to the Mount of Olives" (Mt 26:30). This "hymn" was likely a portion of the so-called Hallel Psalms of the Passover liturgy.[11] Although the Gospels explicitly record no other instance of Jesus singing, we can be sure it was no isolated event. For devout

---

10. John Chrysostom, *Homily on Christmas Morning* (PG 56 col. 385) as quoted in *The Sunday Sermons of the Great Fathers*, vol. 1, trans. M. F. Toal, D.D. (Chicago: Henry Regnery, 1957), p. 111.

11. Psalms 113–118.

Jews accustomed to liturgical singing (especially of the Psalms), it was the normal way to pray.

Pope Benedict imaginatively takes Christ's role here a step further. In the Psalms, Jesus is not only singer, but choirmaster:

> In the Old Testament, [the Psalter] had been considered to be the songs of David; this meant for Christians that these hymns had risen from the heart of the real David, Christ. . . . Christ himself thus becomes the choir director who teaches us the new song and gives the Church the tone and the way in which she can praise God appropriately and blend into the heavenly liturgy."[12]

And it is precisely from the "heavenly liturgy" as depicted in the Book of Revelation that we on earth learn how to sing the new song, and who can sing it. Like all songs, it too requires learning. And as for any "subject," a certain aptitude is required. The challenge lies not in the complexity of score or lyrics, but in its range. The new song demands a breadth reaching into the depths of gratitude and up to the heights of praise for the grace of redemption. As in the Blessed Virgin's Magnificat, it descends into the lowliness of humility while ascending in praise of the Lord's greatness.

12. Benedict XVI, *A New Song for the Lord*, p. 123.

Who can sing it? The Book of Revelation depicts those surrounding the throne of God in heaven as singing "a new song" with this condition: "No one could learn that song except the hundred and forty-four thousand who had been redeemed from the earth" (Rv 14:3).

The main characteristic of the singers is not their exact number (whose value is more symbolic than numerical), but that they have been redeemed and saved. And they know it. The "redeemed from the earth" are those who know what God has done for them. And even while on earth, they respond to the grace of their redemption by living pure and honest lives, following "the Lamb wherever he goes" (cf. Rv 14:4–5).

Revelation further describes these faithful followers as "virgins" or as the "chaste" (cf. Rv 14:4), who sing as they keep step with the Lamb. The Church has always connected this imagery with the religious vocation: a closer, exclusive following of the Lord by those gifted with the grace of embracing chastity, poverty, and obedience. It makes you wonder what their version of the new song sounds like. If on the deepest level a song is a thing of love, then a final word should be said about this special group of people with a very exceptional love song to sing.

These take the new song a step further, from the shores of the Red Sea to the empty sepulcher all the

way to the wedding supper of the Lamb. It is one thing
to sing a hymn of praise and thanksgiving while catching your breath after a hair-raising escape, but quite a
different matter to sing of your nuptials with the Lord
God. One is all about deliverance at the hands of a War-
rior and Hero; the other is a quiet but intense rejoicing
in a permanent espousal with the divine Bridegroom.

Nuns and other types of consecrated women often
hear in Psalm 45 an echo of their own call to wed the
Lord as Brides of Christ. Originally a hymn for a royal
messianic wedding, it naturally lends itself to liturgies
for feasts of the Blessed Virgin. But for women who
model their personal consecration on that of the Virgin, the words are an equally natural accompaniment
to the vowed life. A congregation of Sisters in South-
ern California even has a portion of the first verse
inscribed prominently on the façade of their hospital
chapel: "I sing my works to the king."[13]

> My heart overflows with a goodly theme;
> as I sing my ode to the king,
> my tongue is nimble as the pen of a skillful scribe.
> $(44/45:1)$[14]

---

13. Ps 44:1 (Douay-Rheims version, slightly adapted).

14. This and the subsequent quotations from Ps 44/45 have been
taken from the Confraternity version.

The remainder of the psalm first celebrates the superior dignity of the royal bridegroom, then passes to praise of the "daughter" bride, desired of the king:

Fairer in beauty are you than the sons of men;
grace is poured out upon your lips,
thus God has blessed you forever. (44:3)

Hear, O daughter, and see; turn your ear;
forget your people and your father's house.
So shall the king desire your beauty;
for he is your lord, and you must worship him.

All glorious is the king's daughter as she enters;
her raiment is threaded with spun gold.
In embroidered apparel she is borne in to
the king;
behind her the virgins of her train are brought
to you.
They are borne in with gladness and joy;
they enter the palace of the king. (44:11–16)[15]

The whole scene reads like a solemn liturgical procession: colorful, musical, majestic, scented with "myrrh and aloes and cassia" (v. 8). But at the core of

---

15. Confraternity version.

the grandeur are the hushed tones of voices exchanging vows, the proposal and acceptance of bridegroom and bride. What resonates in a nun's heart is the embarrassing and wonderful disparity between who she is and the majesty of the Lord who makes her his own. She doesn't mind the embarrassment. For the rest of her life, it is a source of wonder and of prayerful reflection, but even more, of praise and thanksgiving. And eternity will not interrupt her song, but sustain it in glorious melody.

This is why the beautiful daughter is told to forget where she has come from, not to dissociate herself from her origins, but to train her focus on the grace of a lifetime embodied in her wedding to the king. A holy forgetting needs to take place, akin to St. Paul's "forgetting what lies behind and straining forward to what lies ahead . . . because Christ Jesus has made me his own" (cf. Phil 3:12–13).

The vocational pattern repeated throughout the Gospels inseparably combines the call to follow Jesus with the demand to leave behind and "forget" even the good things we used to live for. Not always, but in special cases this involves family and friends, and often one's possessions, all of which are good things. But left behind for the sake not only of a better thing, but of the Best:

> But whatever gain I had, I counted as loss for
> the sake of Christ. Indeed I count everything as

loss because of the surpassing worth of knowing Christ Jesus my Lord. For his sake I have suffered the loss of all things, and count them as refuse, in order that I may gain Christ and be found in him. . . . (PHIL 3:7–9A)

Since consecrated religious are called by the Church to "stimulate their brethren by their example,"[16] what we say about this particularly intense form of Christian life should serve to highlight the general, universal call to holiness and union with God, of which religious are the model. "The profession of the evangelical counsels," says the Second Vatican Council, "appears as a sign which can and ought to attract all the members of the Church to an effective and prompt fulfillment of the duties of their Christian vocation."[17]

But prior to modeling fidelity and dutifulness to all the Christian faithful, these special souls should be teachers of songful thanksgiving. Because before anyone takes on their lips a new song of redemption, they have to know what new thing God has done for them, and no one should know this better than those called to belong exclusively to their Redeemer:

---

16. Second Vatican Council, Dogmatic Constitution on the Church: *Lumen Gentium* (November 21, 1964), 2.13, *http://www. vatican.va.*

17. Second Vatican Council, *Lumen Gentium*, 6.43.

I will sing of thy steadfast love,
  O LORD, for ever;
with my mouth I will proclaim thy faithfulness
    to all generations.
For thy steadfast love was established for ever,
  thy faithfulness is firm as the heavens. (Ps 89:1–2)

CHAPTER SEVEN

The Mercies of the Lord Forever

. . . the greater the evil, the more resplendent the wonder of Your mercies. And how many are the reasons I can sing Your mercies forever! I beseech You, my God, that it may be so and that I may sing them without end since You have deigned to bestow upon me mercies so outstanding they amaze those who see them; and as for me, they frequently carry me out of myself to praise You the better.

—St. Teresa of Avila[1]

I f the previous chapter demonstrated the power of sacred song to rekindle memories of salvation history, and even of personal salvation, there is no denying memory's unfortunate power to haunt. Remembrance of God's mercies often becomes a rival in a standoff against loitering memories of sin, shame, and regret.

---

1. Teresa of Avila, *The Book of Her Life*, in *The Collected Works of St. Teresa of Avila*, vol. 1, trans. Kieran Kavanaugh and Otilio Rodriguez, rev. ed. (Washington, D.C.: ICS, 1987), p. 138.

David's anguish for his infamous sin is acute: "For I know my transgressions, and my sin is ever before me" (Ps 51:3). Having one's sins ever before one's eyes is to do a balancing act between hope and despair.

Yet the Psalms assure us of an eternal hymn of praise of God's mercies—already in progress now, awaiting our contribution sooner or later:

> The mercies of the Lord I will sing forever . . .
> For thou hast said: Mercy shall be built up for ever in the heavens. Thy truth shall be prepared in them. (CF. Ps 88:2–3)[2]

And very numerous are the instances in which the Psalter repeats: "Give thanks to the Lord, for he is good, for his mercy endures forever" (Ps 117/118:1).[3] All by itself, Psalm 136 asserts the eternity of God's mercy twenty-six times, once for each of its twenty-six verses. Everything from the creation of the cosmos to the conquest of the Holy Land is counted *mercy*.

Can we reconcile the happiness of heaven with the perpetual recollection of God's mercy? Isn't mercy, after all, love given to the unworthy, the miserable? And aren't those qualities we would much rather forget than

2. Douay version.

3. Confraternity version.

celebrate? If the memory of our sins in this life causes us such grief, why would God allow us to remember them in heaven? Shouldn't our minds be wiped clean of all past wrongs, both those we have committed and those done to us? I have often quoted St. Augustine in these pages as an authority on the Psalms, and it is to him we turn again to help us understand how, even in heaven, the souls of the just could praise the mercies of God.

Coming from the last page of Augustine's monumental work, *The City of God*, we are given a robust picture of eternal praise of the Lord's mercies combined with total stillness, peace, and rest in God. It is hard for us to imagine in this earthly life, with minds brimming over with fears, desires, anxieties—"a soul full of troubles" (cf. Ps 88:3)—that in heaven we will know one thing: God is. And it will be enough. And this prospect should, even here and now, preside over all other concerns.

The passage from the great Doctor deserves a close reading and quoting in full. If the blessed in heaven, he says,

> were not to know that they had been miserable, how could they, as the Psalmist says, "*forever sing the mercies of God*"? Certainly that city shall have no greater joy than the celebration of the grace of Christ, who redeemed us by His blood. There shall be accomplished the words of the Psalm, "*Be still,*

and know that I am God." There shall be the great Sabbath which has no evening, which God celebrated among His first works, as it is written, *"And God rested on the seventh day from all His works which He had made. And God blessed the seventh day, and sanctified it; because that in it He had rested from all His work which God began to make"* (Gn 2:2–3). For we shall ourselves be the seventh day, when we shall be filled and replenished with God's blessing and sanctification.

There shall we be still, and know that He is God; that He is that which we ourselves aspired to be when we fell away from Him, and listened to the voice of the seducer, *"You shall be as gods"* (Gn 3:5), and so abandoned God, who would have made us as gods, not by deserting Him, but by participating in Him. For without Him what have we accomplished, save to perish in His anger? But when we are restored by Him, and perfected with greater grace, we shall have eternal leisure to see that He is God, for we shall be full of Him when He shall be all in all.[4]

Knowing our miseries is the key to eternal praise of mercies, and this is the consensus of the saints, as St. Teresa says ecstatically above about God's "amazing" mercies in her life: "[they] carry me out of myself to

---

4. Augustine, *The City of God*, 22.30.

praise You the better." To be so carried out of oneself in praise that even one's past misdeeds are no cause for shame shows the power of God's grace to engulf even our most dogged feelings of guilt. And if we will have no greater joy than to praise the grace of Christ our redeemer, then whatever we can contribute to that praise will also be a cause for joy—not our sins in themselves, but the grace and mercy that delivered us from them, that reconciled us to God. The focus, in other words, is completely removed from self and placed directly and permanently on God.

The heavenly throne is surrounded not by scores of shamefaced mortals, embarrassed *to be known*, humiliated that everyone knows everything about them. No, the shared feeling is enraptured amazement: "O magnify the LORD with me, and let us exalt his name together!" (Ps 34:3). The celestial air is redolent with choral song; the souls of the saved are all singers, to the last one of them. All are co-celebrants at a banquet to which they have been welcomed by a Host who couldn't bear to celebrate his wedding feast without them.[5] There is a holy "embarrassment" which is very deep gratitude over being the objects of such love, like the royal daughter of Psalm 44, who is encouraged to go confidently to the royal bridegroom, because he desires her beauty.

---

5. Cf. Mt 22:1–14

Gregory of Narek's moving, psalm-like verses tell of the sinner's glorious surprise at being found worthy of admittance to the wedding hall:

> [You] did not dishonor me at your wedding party,
> I, who am unworthy of singing and dancing,
> did not scold me for my disheveled clothes,
> I, who am disorderly,
> did not cast me into the dark, my hands and
> feet shackled.[6]

> Lord of merciful kindness, mighty and
>   victorious . . .
> [i]f you can exchange the abyss for heaven,
> or bring the dark of night into the light,
> if you can turn the bitter bile into sweet manna,
> or the groans of extreme grief
> into the dancing circles at a joyful wedding,
> if for you these are easy and possible,
> then you can do more than these,
> you who reign over all in awesome power.
> To you glory forever and ever.
> Amen.[7]

---

6. Narek, *Speaking with God*, Prayer 5C.

7. Narek, *Speaking with God*, Prayer 29E.

Watchwords such as "wonder" and "amazement" and "awesome" punctuate the outpourings of "earthly" saints, holy ones in transit to paradise, in keeping with the spirit of the Psalter. The psalmist is compelled to proclaim the wonders he has seen, experienced, even only heard about:

Blessed be the LORD,
>for he has wondrously shown his steadfast
>>love to me
>when I was beset as in a besieged city. (Ps 31:21)

Thou hast multiplied, O LORD my God,
>thy wondrous deeds and thy thoughts
>>toward us;
>none can compare with thee!
Were I to proclaim and tell of them,
>they would be more than can be numbered.
>(Ps 40:5)

O God, from my youth thou hast taught me,
>and I still proclaim thy wondrous deeds.
>(Ps 71:17)

On the glorious splendor of thy majesty,
>and on thy wondrous works, I will meditate.
>(Ps 145:5)

Give ear, O my people, to my teaching;
    incline your ears to the words of my mouth!
I will open my mouth in a parable;
    I will utter dark sayings from of old,
things that we have heard and known,
    that our fathers have told us.
We will not hide them from their children,
    but tell to the coming generation
the glorious deeds of the LORD, and his might,
    and the wonders which he has wrought.
    (Ps 78:1–4)

The final picture of all the just souls singing the same new song, joining hands with their saved brethren in the dancing circle, celebrating what God has done for them and for those forever linked to them by the grace and mercy of the Lamb, is simply the transfer to a higher ground of the same rejoicing and praise that should characterize Christian life here below. If God's mercies are numberless, we can do no better than spend our time adding up the ones we can identify, and prayerfully searching out the less obvious ones, greeting each with a word or song of praise.

This really does make a difference in the daily grind—the difference between being self-centered, a "burden to ourselves," or selfless and free to love. Our practical choice becomes either the sinner's "default" of always looking at self and all events as mainly concerning self, or the graced outlook of a child of God, whose gaze is fixed on the Lord:

> Behold, as the eyes of servants
>   look to the hand of their master,
> as the eyes of a maid
>   to the hand of her mistress,
> so our eyes look to the Lord our God,
>   till he have mercy upon us. (Ps 123:2)

The point of mercy is God's goodness and glory. We are all made, so to speak, to be heavenly trophies of divine mercy, living, breathing models of what God can do with sinners who cooperate with his grace. St. Paul's brief summary of mercy in his life captures the idea of prayerful retrospect joined to praise:

> I received mercy for this reason, that in me, as the foremost [of sinners], Jesus Christ might display his perfect patience for an example to those who were to believe in him for eternal life. To the King of ages, immortal, invisible, the only God, be honor and glory for ever and ever. Amen. (1 Tm 1:16–17)

Reflected here is Augustine's assertion that "no greater joy than the celebration of the grace of Christ, who redeemed us by His blood" will characterize heavenly festivity. His reference to Christ's blood not only returns us to the wellspring of divine mercy but points us to its definitive achievement: the purchase of souls for endless beatitude, for perfect joy in the Lord. Entering into the joy of the Lord, we will celebrate the unfailing mercy that drew us by steps and stages, along narrow and unknown paths, to possess the Lamb who laid down his life that we might live in love everlasting.

In these last paragraphs of *The City of God*, Augustine telescopes into a brief, three-act drama the fall of man, redemption in the blood of Christ, and our final and full restoration as the Sabbath *personified*. Recounting human redemption and glorification as an already accomplished fact pacifies the troubled human soul like nothing else. Addled by guilt, regret, and uncertainties over our status before God, how could any of us confidently enter eternity unless we were assured not only of mercy's ultimate triumph, but that our chief glory will be *to have gratefully received divine mercy, to have welcomed merciful treatment*? If mercy is truly God's greatest attribute,[8] then it should be our greatest privilege to sing of it forever.

---

8. "Some theologians affirm that mercy is the greatest of the attributes and perfections of God, and the Bible, Tradition and the whole faith life of the People of God provide particular proofs of this," John Paul II, Encyclical on the Mercy of God *Dives in misericordia* (November 30, 1980), 13, *www.vatican.va.*

I've never forgotten an offhanded remark I once heard in a Roman gift shop, back when I was a seminarian in the Eternal City. Browsing one afternoon in one of the *articoli religiosi* shops around the Vatican, picking out a few devotional articles for friends back home, I overheard a conversation between an American couple who were doing the same for their daughter in the States. In looking for just the right thing, wondering aloud to each other what the young lady would like, their dialogue ran something like this:

"How about a picture of the Divine Mercy?"

"No. She's not really into Divine Mercy."

The remark made me smile, and think: "We don't really have a choice." Mercy is not just a devotion that we can take or leave. It is our only hope for salvation. We heard St. Augustine say earlier: "My whole hope is only in Thy exceeding great mercy."

The tendency to reduce mercy to softhearted indulgence, an easygoing "live and let live" attitude, makes it difficult to explain, for example, the Shepherd who leaves ninety-nine sheep in the wilderness to track down a single stray. And how should we interpret his "rejoicing" at having found the lost sheep? If this is how Jesus describes his relationship with us, we can only conclude that he is not a "detached" God.

Although he respects our freedom to resist him, the Lord is not indifferent. We are not his "private devotion" that he takes up or lays down according to mood. A God who sheds his blood for us is many things, but detached isn't one of them.

Again and again, the Psalms marvel at the glaring disproportion between God's greatness and the care and dignity he lavishes on mankind. The wonder of Psalm 8 is worth quoting in full:

O Lord, our Lord,
how majestic is thy name in all the earth!

Thou whose glory above the heavens is chanted
    by the mouth of babes and infants,
thou hast founded a bulwark because of thy foes,
    to still the enemy and the avenger.

When I look at thy heavens, the work of
        thy fingers,
    the moon and the stars which thou hast
        established;
what is man that thou art mindful of him,
    and the son of man that thou dost care for him?

Yet thou hast made him little less than God,
    and dost crown him with glory and honor.

Thou hast given him dominion over the works
    of thy hands;
  thou hast put all things under his feet,
all sheep and oxen,
    and also the beasts of the field,
the birds of the air, and the fish of the sea,
    whatever passes along the paths of the sea.

O LORD, our LORD,
    how majestic is thy name in all the earth!

If the psalmist questions man's worth at being ele-
vated so high, he doesn't waste time trying to tally the
reasons. The reason is not in man, but in God. And
the dignity that humans certainly possess results from
the share God has given us in his nature. The "answer"
to why God surrounds us with such attention returns
us to the inspired musing of the psalmist, who resolves
everything in the incomparable goodness of God:

I will call to mind the deeds of the LORD;
    yea, I will remember thy wonders of old.
I will meditate on all thy work,
    and muse on thy mighty deeds.
Thy way, O God, is holy.
    What god is great like our God?

Thou art the God who workest wonders,
>   who hast manifested thy might among
>   the peoples. (Ps 77:11–14)

The wonders that prompt such amazement in the speaker are only another way of identifying mercies. He is attentive to them. Regularly praying with the Psalms also sensitizes us to what God is doing in our lives, especially when his providence is not so easy to recognize. We tend to notice divine interventions only when we are aware of an exceptional need for help or forgiveness. But nothing about us escapes the notice of him who numbers the hairs of our head. And this has far-reaching consequences.

When Jesus compares disciples to netted fish, to birds protected in the branches of a large, shady tree, or to the sheep of a guarded fold, then the implication is clear. Fallen people are prone to stray and need to be guided, protected, often even rescued. This is what God's mercy does.

It might take something like the riches-to-rags experience of the prodigal son to bring some straying souls back to God. That the famous wanderer of the parable only came to his senses standing over a pig-sty, coveting the slop the swine fed on, proves that whatever means God can use to reach our hearts is fair game. Whether the stench of garbage or the fragrance of a rose garden, all is mercy. Beauty or ugliness, joy or sorrow, can serve as the lever that detaches the heart from harmful ways and leads it back into the ways of salvation. Who hasn't experienced this?

This is why St. John Paul II, although encouraging us never to tire in approaching the Lord, yet adds a note of caution. He warns against our awful ability to limit what God's mercy can do:

> Mercy in itself, as a perfection of the infinite God, is also infinite. Also infinite therefore and inexhaustible is the Father's readiness to receive the prodigal children who return to His home. Infinite are the readiness and power of forgiveness which flow continually from the marvelous value of the sacrifice of the Son. No human sin can prevail over this power or even limit it. On the part of man only a lack of good will can limit it, a lack of readiness to be converted and to repent, in other words persistence in obstinacy, opposing grace and truth, especially in the face of the witness of the cross and resurrection of Christ.[9]

Opposing grace and truth sounds like something we would never do. But in the face of life's setbacks, we are often tempted to. When grace doesn't "look" like grace

---

9. John Paul II, *Dives in misericordia*, 13.

and truth hurts, our instinct as fallen people is to turn away and ignore the mercy contained in contradiction. This is why John Paul II underscores "the witness of the cross and resurrection of Christ." Jesus risen from the dead changes everything: how we see the world, ourselves, our neighbor, good and evil, justice and injustice; how we live and love; how we hope and believe.

It is worth noting here that our Lord's post-resurrection teaching was directed to disciples whose minds needed to be opened, and eyes enlightened, to see what grace and mercy had accomplished through the injustice of his death. And standing tall among the Old Testament Scriptures cited by him is the Book of Psalms: "everything written about me in the law of Moses and the prophets and the psalms must be fulfilled" (Lk 24:44). In the light of the Resurrection, we can read such difficult psalm passages as the following and begin to see a larger mercy contained even in the adversity the Lord permits for us:

> Let the just man strike me; that is kindness;
>> let him reprove me; it is oil for my head,
>>> which my head will not refuse,
> but I will pray under these afflictions.
>> (Ps 140/141:5)[10]

---

10. Confraternity version.

In eternity, in the eternal light of God, we will see all things in him, including our sins, and the place they had in his providence—because even these have a place. St. Augustine insists on this point, and we need to as well: even the sins of those whom God calls to himself are resolved providentially for their salvation and sanctification. Citing St. Paul,[11] Augustine affirms that for those who love God, "God co-operates with all things for good; *really, absolutely all things*, so that even if any of them go astray, and turn aside from the right path, even this itself God makes to profit them for good, so that they return more humble and more instructed."[12]

That is an encouraging truth for those whose track record is a source of nagging regret and shame. But whether we have little or much to make up for, the assurance that God can ultimately make right what we have done wrong relieves the soul of a sense of irreparable harm caused by sin. It also tells us that God is not simply a great "mastermind" who knows how to make beautiful artwork out of rubbish, or to assemble a complicated puzzle blindfolded. Instead, God does these things because he is merciful. There is no need to complicate that.

---

11. Cf. Rm 8:28–30.

12. Augustine, *De correptione et gratia*, 24. Emphasis added.

Gracious is the LORD, and righteous;
  our God is merciful.
The LORD preserves the simple;
  when I was brought low, he saved me.
Return, O my soul, to your rest;
  for the LORD has dealt bountifully with you.
  (Ps 116:5–7)

Steadying our eyes on the fixed point of God's merciful love steadies our steps in the precarious balancing act of remembrance and remorse:

For thy steadfast love is before my eyes,
  and I walk in faithfulness to thee. (Ps 26:3)

I lift up my eyes to the hills.
  From whence does my help come?
My help comes from the LORD,
  who made heaven and earth.

He will not let your foot be moved. . . .
  (Ps 121:1–3)

Habitually training our gaze on the Lord is the point of remembering the saving moments on the timeline of sacred history. Different from nostalgia, which often romanticizes the irretrievable past, a remembrance of sacred events actually makes them present *in power*. That is, God's saving power manifested at certain junctures in salvation history is mystically or sacramentally "tapped into" in the present.

> Be mindful of thy mercy, O LORD, and of thy
>   steadfast love,
>   for they have been from of old.
> Remember not the sins of my youth, or my
>   transgressions;
>   according to thy steadfast love remember me,
>   for thy goodness' sake, O LORD! (Ps 25:6–7)

The very fact that such a prayer can be made at all is proof positive against whatever lingering doubts may fetter us in the present. Obviously, the speaker's sins continue as bad memories. But notice: he first invokes the timelessness of God's mercy and steadfast love as surety against his own irreversible sins. God is faithful from of old and his fidelity, like his mercy, endures forever.

The Church's sacred liturgy employs the technical term "anamnesis" to describe the liturgical recollection of (particularly) Christ's redemptive mission and the events of the Paschal Mystery. The Eucharistic Prayer is the special locus of liturgical review of God's saving actions. In the Roman Rite, Eucharistic Prayer IV is especially rich in evoking not only Jesus' mission but salvation history as a whole. And every "Collect," or opening prayer, of the Mass does the same thing: it asks for a grace here and now based on a past saving event or the merits of a saint. This helps to keep our focus where it belongs not only at Mass, but even beyond it.

If God's past fidelity to his people, his willingness to save, connects us to his power in the particular struggles of daily life, then we need to be keyed into it *all the time.* Saints throughout the ages have used the Psalms for this purpose. The so-called Desert Fathers (and Mothers) of the third- and fourth-century Egyptian monastic settlements are among the most famous for basing their private prayer on the Psalms. These they memorized through continual recitation—praying them as they worked, traveled, and faced temptations of various kinds.

You could call this *applied psalmody,* i.e., wielding the Psalter as the God-given weapon it is to shield oneself against the darts of the enemy. And even more than protection, the Psalms can lift our attention and affection out of the trenches of temptation and into the heavenly choirs of praise and thanksgiving. Nothing so overcomes the nag of negative, self-defeating thoughts than the effort to lift up our hearts to him who sits enthroned over the tempest (cf. Ps 29:10). Since all temptation mixes something good with deception, we need to live in the truth and remind ourselves of the truth when lies are about to swamp our boats.

Psalms verses, and other shorter prayers, were for the ancient monks often regarded as "javelins," to be hurled quickly and forcefully in the face of desperate trials and temptations. There comes a breaking point for everyone where a temptation does more than annoy: it insists, it demands. And people have to be equally insistent in their prayer to God. A story recounted among the sayings of the Desert Fathers underscores this need not only to punctuate the day with prayer, but to make one's life a continual prayer:

> The blessed Epiphanius, Bishop of Cyprus, was told this by the abbot of a monastery which he had in Palestine, "By your prayers we do not neglect our appointed round of psalmody, but we are very careful to recite Terce, Sext and None." Then Epiphanius corrected them with the following comment, "It is clear that you do not trouble about the other hours of the day, if you cease from prayer. The true monk should have prayer and psalmody continually in his heart."[13]

---

13. Benedicta Ward, SLG, trans., *The Sayings of the Desert Fathers: The Alphabetical Collection* (Collegeville, Minn.: Liturgical Press, 1984), p. 57.

Evagrius of Pontus (345–399) even compiled a kind of handbook of biblical verses to be used against the various assaults of demons.[14] Countering evil suggestions, such as acting out in lust, avarice, or pride, one could do no better than follow the example of Jesus. He refuted each of his three temptations with a Scripture verse. It should come as no surprise that the vast majority of references in this unique manual come from the Psalter.

Evagrius offers, for example, a verse to fend off sadness and also one to repel lust:

> 30. Against the thoughts that advise us to flee from before the demons' evil and not oppose them valiantly in the contest:
>
>> In the Lord I have placed my trust. How will you say to my soul, "Flee to the mountains as a sparrow"? (Ps 10:1)[15]
>
> 26. Against the soul that supposes that the thoughts of fornication are more powerful than God's commandments, which were given to us for the extirpation of this passion:

---

14. Evagrius of Pontus, *Talking Back* (*Antirrhêtikos*): *A Monastic Handbook for Combating Demons*, trans. David Brakke (Collegeville, Minn.: Liturgical Press, 2009).

15. Evagrius of Pontus, p. 106.

> I will beat them like the dust before the wind,
> and I will grind them like the mud of the
> streets. (Ps 17:43)[16]

One of the desert "Mothers," Amma Syncletica (c. 270–350), once said about the usefulness of "prayer and psalmody" against the crippling sadness and discouragement induced by the devil:

> 'There is grief that is useful, and there is grief that is destructive. The first sort consists in weeping over one's own faults and weeping over the weakness of one's neighbors, in order not to destroy one's purpose, and attach oneself to the perfect good. But there is also a grief that comes from the enemy, full of mockery, which some call accidie.[17] This spirit must be cast out, mainly by prayer and psalmody.'[18]

Knowing certain psalms by heart, or at least several pertinent phrases, puts on our lips a potent antidote against discouragement or fear, enabling us to confront the challenge before us with confidence in the Lord. Additionally, it arms us with an airtight rebuttal against the attacks of the devil. Christian tradition has

---

16. Evagrius of Pontus, p. 75.

17. Or *acedia*, a word denoting spiritual melancholy that drains a person of his motivation to pursue holiness.

18. Ward, *The Sayings of the Desert Fathers*, p. 235.

always seen the repeated cries of the psalmist for deliverance from his enemies not so much as a military conflict as a demonic one. The enemy, the "Accuser," can build a pretty convincing case against us. He's been an eyewitness to all of our worst moments. We cannot deny the allegations made against us. We can only appeal to mercy. Case closed. We win, because Christ has won for us.

The psalmist is continually beseeching God to remember his saving deeds of old that he, or the people of God, might be saved here and now:

> O God, why dost thou cast us off for ever?
>> Why does thy anger smoke against the sheep
>>> of thy pasture?
> Remember thy congregation, which thou hast
>> gotten of old,
>> which thou hast redeemed to be the tribe
>>> of thy heritage!
>> Remember Mount Zion, where thou hast
>>> dwelt. (Ps 74:1–2)

> I cry aloud to God,
>> aloud to God, that he may hear me.
> In the day of my trouble I seek the Lord;
>> in the night my hand is stretched out
>>> without wearying;
>> my soul refuses to be comforted.

I think of God, and I moan;
   I meditate, and my spirit faints.

I consider the days of old,
   I remember the years long ago.
I commune with my heart in the night;
   I meditate and search my spirit:
"Will the Lord spurn forever,
   and never again be favorable?
Has his steadfast love for ever ceased?
   Are his promises at an end for all time?
Has God forgotten to be gracious?
   Has he in anger shut up his compassion?"
And I say, "It is my grief
   that the right hand of the Most High has
      changed."

I will call to mind the deeds of the Lord;
   yea, I will remember thy wonders of old.
   (Ps 77:1–3, 5–11)

I remember the days of old,
   I meditate on all that thou hast done;
   I muse on what thy hands have wrought.
I stretch out my hands to thee;
   my soul thirsts for thee like a parched land.

Make haste to answer me, O LORD!
   My spirit fails!
Hide not thy face from me,
   lest I be like those who go down to the Pit.
   (Ps 143:5–7)

Arise, O LORD; O God, lift up thy hand;
   forget not the afflicted. (Ps 10:12)

Invoking God's precedent of saving justifies present expectation of deliverance. But there is obviously
no question of nostalgia here, of recalling a golden age
when all was ideal. No, such impassioned prayers reflect
the reality of bad situations from which people needed
to be saved. Salvation is all about the unideal (those
lacking ideals or qualities), the fallen-through, the
defective, the sick and disordered, who are *made right*
by One who has the power to save. Setting our sights
there, and there only, makes the difference between
intractable hopelessness and undefeatable hope.

The recalling of past sins, then, cannot be blamed
for despair. Rather, putting an unchristian spin on
them sinks the soul.

The suicide of Judas Iscariot is the iconic case in
point. His extreme "sorrow unto death"[19] resulted not

---

19. Cf. Sir 38:17–18; 2 Cor 7:10.

from legitimate grief over his betrayal of Christ. His sin was undeniable and certainly merited the greatest possible remorse. But the hopelessness that gave birth to suicide came from an implicit assumption unfortunately shared by many: that people have to undo or erase the past if they would ever enjoy peace and reconciliation again. That is the unchristian slant that undoes the work of grace in our lives. Grace exists in the present moment, and is reparative, restorative. Our new life in Christ is not mere retrieval, recapturing lost ground. Not *recovery*, but *rebirth*.

But isn't this a temptation for us all? Our inner peace seems to depend upon the impossible: undoing an episode of our personal history. Newman sees at the root of this yearning to erase, forget, to get back where we started from and start over in innocence, a deep longing for Eden.[20] He astutely links our fondness for our own childhood with the spiritual longing for the state of innocence, or our natural state of being, the state of existence we were created for.

> Therefore we may well look back on the garden of Eden, as we would on our own childhood. That childhood is a type of the perfect Christian state; our Saviour so made it when He said that we must

20. John Henry Newman, "The State of Innocence," in *Parochial and Plain Sermons*, pp. 1014–1023.

become as little children to enter His kingdom. Yet it too is a thing past and over. We are not, we cannot be children; grown men have faculties, passions, aims, principles, views, duties, which children have not; still, however, we must become *as* little children; in them we are bound to see Christian perfection, and to labour for it with them in our eye. Indeed there is a very much closer connexion between the state of Adam in Paradise and our state in childhood, than may at first be thought; so that in surveying Eden, we are in a way looking back on our own childhood; and in aiming to be children again, we are aiming to be as Adam on his creation.[21]

It's not hard to see Newman's point. To return and inhabit the simple and friendly landscape of Eden, where Adam and Eve lived in communion with God and each other, speaks to the world-weariness of adult life. And even more, to youthful days misspent and now repented. Isn't there at least one sin for us all that sits like dead weight on the heart, never to be lifted or shouldered by another?

But we don't need a time machine. We don't need to continually revisit the past with regret. What we need is to fix our gaze in the present on God's mercy. "We need constantly to contemplate the mystery of mercy,"

21. Newman.

Pope Francis exhorted us at the outset of *Misericordiae vultus*, the Bull of Indiction for the extraordinary Jubilee of Mercy, implying how no Christian can think or speak about God's mercy in a purely detached way:

> It is a wellspring of joy, serenity, and peace. Our salvation depends on it. Mercy: the ultimate and supreme act by which God comes to meet us. Mercy: the bridge that connects God and man, opening our hearts to the hope of being loved forever despite our sinfulness.[22]

Woven throughout the entirety of our lives is this love that can't be reduced to an *ad hoc*, as-needed remedy for when we've really messed up things. If mercy were only that, it would hardly merit a yearlong celebration, much less an eternal one: "Forever will I sing the mercies of the Lord."

If mercy deserves everlasting praise, if the blessed in heaven chant it as their perpetual *new song*, then it must be a reality shaping my life even now, from cradle to grave. If mercy, above all, seeks to dispel the miseries of others as though they were one's own,[23] then God's mercy must be a daily reminder to me of the

---

22. Cf. Francis, Bull of Indiction of the Extraordinary Jubilee of Mercy *Misericordiae vultus* (April 11, 2015), 2, www.vatican.va.

23. Cf. Thomas Aquinas, *Summa Theologiae*, 1.21.3.

price that he has paid to take away my worst miseries: "But God, who is rich in mercy, out of the great love with which he loved us, even when we were dead through our trespasses, made us alive together with Christ" (Eph 2:4–5).

Anticipating our steps, accommodating our errors, removing obstacles or permitting them for our good, mercy rids us of the real miseries that prevent us from arriving at the goal of our existence: everlasting enjoyment of God. But since the road to perfect joy is narrow, much tangled overgrowth needs clearing so that we can travel safely home. Sin, sinful attitudes, self-defeating and distracting desires—all need to be removed or righted. Mercy accomplishes this, relieving us of the unbearable weight of sin and guilt through forgiveness, while rendering us capable of face-to-face enjoyment of infinite goodness.

You Have Enlarged My Heart

Love Changed & Renewed

> I will run the way of your commands, for you have enlarged my heart.
>
> —Psalm 118/119:32[1]

L ife and love are inseparable for Christians. They either grow together or they die together. The promise "Do this and you will live" from the lips of Jesus illustrates the connection: if we want to live fully, we must love rightly. To keep his commands is not only to obey; it is to love: "If you love me, you will keep my commandments" (Jn 14:15). Life in Christ increases in proportion to love, which is the umbilical

---

1. My own translation of a simple verse from the Latin Vulgate Bible: "*viam mandatorum tuorum curram quoniam dilatasti cor meum*" (Ps 118:32).

cord of Christian life, not only nourishing but conveying a share in the life of God, who is Love.

That we have actually begun to live a new life in Christ is shown when our love has also become new. This is sometimes a stumbling block for converts as well as lifelong Christians: Christian faith is not simply an add-on to a life that's already decent and respectable. Christianity isn't the icing on the cake. If new life in Christ is going to mean more than joining an organization with bylaws to observe and dues to pay, the newness needs to come from within us. God needs to put it there. He needs to redirect our lives by redirecting our love.

We want to end up at a love that consumes. Setting the bar any lower is an unworthy downgrade for us who are expected to grow *perfect* in love.[2] To be consumed by anything can simply mean being obsessive, at one extreme, or at the opposite pole, wholeheartedly devoted. An addict is consumed just as much as a saint, and this is no contradiction. In fact, the two have the most important thing in common: love. Both can't get by without something—a substance for one, God for the other. Neither can imagine life without the object of his or her desire. And there is much more to this than meets the eye.

---

2. Cf. 1 Jn 2:5, 4:12, 4:17–18.

The bulk of ongoing Christian conversion, of submitting to gospel love as our guiding yoke, means redirecting our love toward its highest Object. Newman describes this as the normal progression of holiness. Conversion and growth in holiness have nothing to do with stamping love out of the human heart, nothing to do with snuffing out our emotions. God makes a saint out of sinner by using the very equipment he gave us in creating us human:

> He takes him as he is, and uses him against himself: He turns his affections into another channel, and extinguishes a carnal love by infusing a heavenly charity. . . . [I]t is the very triumph of His grace, that He enters into the heart of man, and persuades it, and prevails with it, while He changes it.[3]

The heart that God enlarges is this one described by Newman: built of love, affections, and passions, yet in need of grace to find its focus. The psalmist's acclamation "Thy word is a lamp to my feet and a light to my path" (Ps 119:105) has more to do with steering the heart than plotting footsteps. But notice how God attracts to a higher love by entering the heart,

---

3. John Henry Newman, "Purity and Love," in *Discourses Addressed to Mixed Congregations* (London: Longmans, Green, and Co., 1899), p. 71.

"extinguishing" its unholy fires by proposing a loftier ideal, and gently persuading it to change. Pressure, threats, and fear have power only to compel a forced march, not inspire the light step of the runner along the way of love.

Not a few men have turned away from lustful habits after having been stopped in their tracks by a beautiful image of our Lady. Many women have desisted from serial relationships after an encounter with the Sacred Heart. God appeals to our best and noblest desires for love, so that the inferior product begins to look like refuse beside it. Once St. Paul had been touched by Christ, he could say this without blinking: "I have suffered the loss of all things, and count them as refuse, in order that I may gain Christ" (Phil 3:8). This is the divine strategy at work.

We all have, as Newman also says, a "ruling principle,"[4] and it should come as no surprise that that principle is always love. We are all lovers of something, and the real problem is not that we have no love but that our "affections do not rest on Almighty God as their great Object."[5] Where they *do* rest is revealing, and becomes the "X marks the spot" of the gospel: "For where your treasure is, there will your heart be also"

4. John Henry Newman, "Love, the One Thing Needful," in *Parochial and Plain Sermons*, pp. 1156.

5. Newman.

(Mt 6:21). Where heart and treasure intersect, there you find the power station that runs a person's life.

Consider the alignment of heart and treasure in Psalm 63. The speaker is so consumed by God that he claims his love as eclipsing even life itself:

O God, thou art my God, I seek thee,
  my soul thirsts for thee;
my flesh faints for thee,
  as in a dry and weary land where no water is.
So I have looked upon thee in the sanctuary,
  beholding thy power and glory.
Because thy steadfast love is better than life,
  my lips will praise thee.
So I will bless thee as long as I live;
  I will lift up my hands and call on thy name.

My soul is feasted as with marrow and fat,
  and my mouth praises thee with joyful lips,
when I think of thee upon my bed,
  and meditate on thee in the watches of the night;
for thou hast been my help,
  and in the shadow of thy wings I sing for joy.
My soul clings to thee;
  thy right hand upholds me.

Does this seem to go too far? Thirsting, fainting, pondering the beloved at night, clinging to him, even regarding vocal praise as a savory meal? No, this is the language of love, which no one finds silly or extreme when actually experiencing it. Whether romantic or divine, love tends to spark a kind of "crazy talk" that, only in the case of God, will never be crazy enough, go far enough, or say all there is about him. The Lord is the lone exception to the rule that all love cools over time. With him, the fire continues to climb, the thirst to deepen, the longing to intensify.

A woman once shared with me an unusual difficulty with her husband. He felt annoyed and neglected because she had begun spending more time in prayer and had become increasingly involved in her parish. She was undergoing a deeper conversion, but her husband wasn't prepared to keep pace with her. At wit's end, he finally told her, "You know what your problem is? You love God more than you love me!" His criticism was more insightful than he probably knew. In reality, you can't love God too much. And unless we love God with all our heart, mind, and strength, we won't do a very good job of loving our neighbor. God alone is love. We are only borrowers.

It is easy to go wrong in seeking love and happiness. "After all," St. Josemaría observes, "the world has many good things to offer that attract our hearts, which crave happiness and anxiously run in search of love."[6] Yet to desire happiness and hurry after love is, at root, holy. God himself sparks the search in creating us as restless and incomplete beings without him. Often he even leads souls along a path of lesser loves that serve as clues to the true treasure. Fine arts, gardening, sports, and many other, and stranger, interests have been known to land people on the mound of the treasure buried in a field.

Ps 118:32 makes clear ("I will run the way of your commands, for you have enlarged my heart") that God must do something to our hearts before we can not only find the right path to love, but hasten on it without stumbling. The love of God reforms us by changing both what and how we love. As said above, this is Christian conversion in a nutshell. This is also what the old covenant promise of a new heart and a new spirit accomplishes: "A new heart I will give you, and a new spirit I will put within you; and I will take out of your flesh the heart of stone and give you a heart of flesh" (Ez 36:26).

The stony quality of the human heart is replaced by one tender enough to be literally *impressed* by God's law and love, like wax that receives the indelible impression of a king's signet ring:

6. Escrivá, *Friends of God*, no. 209.

> . . . this is the covenant which I will make with
> the house of Israel after those days, says the Lord:
> I will put my law within them, and I will write it
> upon their hearts; and I will be their God, and they
> shall be my people. . . . (Jer 31:33)

The enlarging of the heart and running of the lover demonstrates the cause-and-effect between what God does for us and what he makes us capable of doing in return: He gives us a new heart large enough to *run* in the way of his commands. We run, we hurry, not to attain just any old thing but only the best things. God must be doing something to our hearts to make them want him as a panting deer longs for flowing streams, as "obsessively" as the one who meditates on him day and night: even seven times a day, and not excluding rising at midnight in praise.[7]

Frequent are the psalmist's urgent cries for God to "hurry" and "make haste" to help in times of distress:

> Be pleased, O God, to deliver me!
>> O Lord, make haste to help me! (Ps 70:1)
>
> O God, be not far from me;
>> O my God, make haste to help me! (Ps 71:12)

---

7. Cf. Psalms 42:1–2; 1:2; 119:62, 164.

But haste and hurry are also irreplaceable on our side. St. Paul's exhortation to "run" so as to obtain the "prize" of everlasting life is well-known (cf. 1 Cor 9:23–27). No less noteworthy is the bride's impatience for her beloved in the Song of Solomon: "Draw me after you, let us make haste. The king has brought me into his chambers" (Song 1:4). Love is the only thing that makes people run. Love is the draw. St. Augustine offers this charmingly simple example:

> You hold out a green twig to a sheep, and you draw it. Nuts are shown to a child, and he is attracted; he is drawn by what he runs to, drawn by loving it, drawn without hurt to the body, drawn by a cord of the heart. If, then, these things, which among earthly delights and pleasures are shown to them that love them, draw them, since it is true that "*every man is drawn by his own pleasure*," does not Christ, revealed by the Father, draw?[8]

Christian life hits its stride when love is felt to be an urgent and compelling need, as when Jesus says of his mission: "I came to cast fire upon the earth; and would that it were already kindled! I have a baptism to

---

    8. Augustine, *Tractates on John*, 26.5, *NPNF: First Series*, vol. 7, p. 170. Wording slightly modernized. This public domain work can be accessed at *www.newadvent.org*.

be baptized with; and how I am constrained until it is accomplished!" (Lk 12:49–50). But getting up to the speed of that stride, even to the velocity of a wildfire, is where many of us fall flat. From starting gate to immediate face-plant is as far as many of us seem to get, or at least that's how it might feel.

This deserves a closer look.

That our love does not keep pace with what we do, that our good works often seem to be done in a purely mechanical way, is the frustration of very many sincere Christians who seek spiritual direction. "I feel like I'm just going through the motions," or "How do I know if I'm doing these things for the love of God?" are common self-criticisms. To be honest, it's not always easy to tell, at least not at the beginning. Perseverance is often the most telling gauge, since no one lasts in God's service except those who serve for him, and not for the benefits of religion.[9]

But for the time being, people can at least relieve themselves of the burden of not knowing. If God wanted us to know everything at once, with perfect clarity, he would shine that light into our minds from the get-go. Some ignorance about our spiritual state is good for us. God's purpose is not to confuse, but to engender trust in people who normally want to have

9. Cf. 1 Tm 6:3–10.

all the answers, and who stop depending when they do. In the Christian life, it's either walk by faith and trust or don't walk at all.

As the psalmist takes stock of the darkness surrounding him, faith and trust lift him above it:

> Light rises in the darkness for the upright;
>> the Lord is gracious, merciful, and righteous.
>> (Ps 112:4)

> Then they cried to the Lord in their trouble,
>> and he delivered them from their distress;
> he brought them out of darkness and gloom,
>> and broke their bonds asunder.
> Let them thank the Lord for his steadfast love,
>> for his wonderful works to the sons of men!
>> (Ps 107:13–15)

If we are honest with ourselves, we know that we can stick with almost anything in view of a reward. Endurance that repays our efforts is attractive—from schooling to exercise to overcoming substance abuse—all have a particular payoff that makes the sweat worth it. The patriarch Jacob is the classic biblical example. He agreed to a seven-year workload to earn the hand of the beautiful Rachel, but the years "seemed to him but a few days because of the love he had for her"

(Gn 29:20). And we will do likewise if the goal is compelling enough.

But it is in the absence of any tangible prize that motives begin their purification. Then such questions surface as, "What for? Why should I care? Is it worth the trouble?" And a choice presents itself: keep doing it for God, to serve him and save souls, or quit and seek our pleasures elsewhere. The latter is more or less a dead end, another escape from both self and God. Everyone needs his or her motives purified, to some degree. But it is spiritually counterproductive to keep substituting one work for another on the grounds that a payoff is not forthcoming. We all know people who pass from one job or hobby or interest to another, as soon as one becomes boring or unrewarding. In the Christian life, a very different economy of labor and harvest exists:

> So neither he who plants nor he who waters is anything, but only God who gives the growth. He who plants and he who waters are equal, and each shall receive his wages according to his labor. For we are God's fellow workers. . . . (1 Cor 3:7–9)

The love that enlarges the heart to run needs to overcome the natural craving for countable, measurable results. Otherwise we won't manage to run in the way of love without tripping all over ourselves, if not turning back altogether. The Lord is more than willing to provide incentives as needed, such as encouragement or praise from others, generous fundraising for worthy projects, or even good publicity. But no saint ever based his or her mission solely on having something to show for it. The lives of the saints often record a very different story of failures, misunderstandings, and rejection. Yet the fruit, because it is God's, inevitably comes.

The psalmist sometimes must sit in darkness and feel utterly perplexed by the ways of God, yet stays faithful to him. Why? Not out of routine, custom, or force of habit. Not because he's too timid to strike out on his own. Rather, it is the simple conviction of being loved that keeps him in place, on track, singing, and ready to wait:

> Blessed be God,
>   because he has not rejected my prayer
> or removed his steadfast love from me! (Ps 66:20)

> Wait for the LORD;
>   be strong, and let your heart take courage;
>   yea, wait for the LORD! (Ps 27:14)

> Be still before the LORD, and wait patiently
>   for him. . . . (Ps 37:7)

How can we run without stumbling or back-tracking? We need to be loved first. "The Psalms do not tell us not to love," comments St. Augustine, "but to choose the object of our love. But how can we choose unless we are first chosen? We cannot love unless someone has loved us first."[10] Commenting on Psalm 149, he continues:

> Listen to the apostle John: *We love him, because he first loved us.* The source of man's love for God can only be found in the fact that God loved him first. He has given us himself as the object of our love, and he has also given us its source. What this source is you may learn more clearly from the apostle Paul who tells us: *The love of God has been poured into our hearts.* This love is not something we generate ourselves; it comes to us through the Holy Spirit who has been given to us (Rm 5:5).[11]

Psalm 149 is a rallying cry to praise, sing, make music, and dance, from one who knows himself, and his people, to be specially loved:

---

10. Augustine, Commentary on Psalm 149, Sermon 34 (Sermo 34.1–3, 5–6; CCL 41, 424–426): *http://www.vatican.va/spirit/documents/spirit_20010508_agostino-vescovo_en.html.*

11. Augustine.

Praise the LORD!
Sing to the LORD a new song,
   his praise in the assembly of the faithful!
Let Israel be glad in his Maker,
   let the sons of Zion rejoice in their King!
Let them praise his name with dancing,
   making melody to him with timbrel and lyre!
For the LORD takes pleasure in his people;
   he adorns the humble with victory.
Let the faithful exult in glory;
   let them sing for joy on their couches.
Let the high praises of God be in their throats
   and two-edged swords in their hands,
to wreak vengeance on the nations
   and chastisement on the peoples,
to bind their kings with chains
   and their nobles with fetters of iron,
to execute on them the judgment written!
   This is glory for all his faithful ones.
Praise the LORD!

Love's origin can only be God, who is Love: "In this is love, not that we loved God but that he loved us" (1 Jn 4:10). But even to trace something back to its origin is not the same as to know it personally, intimately.

I might know who a man's parents are without knowing the first thing about what makes him tick. But to make us understand or *know* love, God takes a concrete action, creates an event by which he reveals his inner nature: "By this we know love, that he laid down his life for us" (1 Jn 3:16).

People do not love abstract things in a personal and passionate way. But a man's body and blood given for me? I get that. And if I have any understanding at all, I will love it. I will adore it. I will seek to imitate it. But before I do any of that, I will sit still long enough to let it work on me. I will first be loved by him, through his sacrifice for me: "I live by faith in the Son of God, who loved me and gave himself for me" (Gal 2:20).

Those who strain to love God but who nevertheless stumble along, need to revisit the beginning, the Alpha of all love. We need to be still before the Lord and let him love us. Psalm 127 condemns as "vain" the efforts of those who rise early and toil if the Lord is not the inspiration behind their labors. The psalm furthers the point: God even pours gifts on his loved ones while they sleep.[12]

Awareness of being loved is the only power that can change us in any lasting and meaningful way. Absence of this conviction, even the absence of the desire for

---

12. Cf. Ps 127:1–5.

the conviction, makes it virtually impossible for one to wait for the Lord and trust in him, much less to run in the way of his commands. Yet it would be a mistake to imagine that our feelings or thoughts have the power to make God's love present. In fact, that is to place yet another psychological and emotional burden on ourselves. No, his love is already here, already at work. Our task is simply to open our hearts to it. The Lord calls us to accept with great humility our vocation as the object of his love.

Few have expressed this in as heartfelt a way as St. Elizabeth of the Trinity, just days before she died in 1906. In a short letter to her prioress, amounting to a kind of last will and testament, the dying Carmelite assured her spiritual mother:

> "*You are uncommonly loved*," loved by that love of preference that the Master had here below for some and which brought them so far. He does not say to you as to Peter: "Do you love Me more than these?" Mother, listen to what He tells you: "*Let* yourself be loved more than these! That is, without fearing that any obstacle will be a hindrance to it, for I am free to pour out My love on whom I wish! '*Let* yourself be loved more than these' is your vocation. It is in being faithful to it that you will make Me happy, for you will magnify the power

of my love. This love can rebuild what you have destroyed. *Let* yourself be loved more than these."[13]

People sometimes say that about themselves in the context of spiritual direction: "I'm not letting God love me. I think I just need to let God love me." What does that mean? To me it always sounds like an individual's vague sense of resisting the Lord by objecting to or recoiling from the circumstances he permits in his or her life. In translation, it could just as easily mean: *I'm too worried and fearful, too controlling. I can't surrender to what God wills for my life, so I try to bend everything to conform to my preferences. And it never works. My heart feels hard. My mind seems closed. I feel trapped.*

If letting yourself be loved means cherishing a conviction that God has a special love for you, then you will be on the lookout for expressions of that love coming from all sides. You won't be so caught off guard or put off by the unexpected. You may even find that people and situations that previously annoyed you suddenly open up to you as God's instruments. Because you are growing in love, you see events and people more from the perspective of love. No longer from the perspective of fear, anger, helplessness—but of love.

13. Elizabeth of the Trinity, "Let Yourself Be Loved," in *The Complete Works*, p. 179.

The people who complain of not letting God love them are also admitting that they are allowing something else to rule their lives. If the Lord is not the Master of my life, then I am probably too afraid to give him control of it. I cannot wait in patience with the psalmist, my eyes trained on God, because I cannot endure the uncertainty of waiting in faith and hope.

As we mentioned in an earlier chapter, our inherited distrust of God—passed on to us from Adam and Eve—needs to be healed, and trust rebuilt. We make so many decisions out of a lack of trust in God, from a desire for self-protection, that we undermine the very foundations of our spiritual lives: "And without faith it is impossible to please him. For whoever would draw near to God must believe that he exists and that he rewards those who seek him" (Heb 11:6).

Whatever wreckage our bad choices may have produced, however distrust may have distanced us from God and tangled our spiritual lives, St. Elizabeth assures us: "This love can rebuild what you have destroyed." Only God's love *surrendered to* can rebuild us. The Lord is constantly taking human error, human sin, and weaving it into the wonderful tapestry of his providence. Even the worst events in world history and in our individual lives are accounted for. My surrender to God repairs, renews, and rebuilds what I have destroyed through sin, laziness, self-indulgence, fear, and so forth. God takes into his hands all of the broken pieces and refashions them into something more beautiful than if it had never been fractured.

This can be very hard to believe. But a contemplative look at the crucifix should remove all doubt. The broken body of Christ is the most eloquent sign of God's power to renew in the midst of chastisement and injury, even trauma. The risen body of Christ, healed and glorious, is made even more beautiful by the violence it willingly endured in the Passion, because that violence was borne out of the highest love. A mangled body horrifies. It is a spectacle from which people normally turn their faces, seeing no beauty, perceiving nothing attractive or desirable. Yet when you recognize this as the Man who took your sins away, you might find yourself falling to your knees and beginning to heal.[14]

God does not love sin, but he loves us even as we are sinning. God does not smile upon evil, but he loves those who do the evil. This makes no sense at all if we think of love sentimentally, as nothing more than mutual good feelings. Our sins don't make God *feel good*. But if we understand love as God presents it to us, we see a love whose sole intent is to save

---

14. Cf. Is 53, the so-called "Fourth Servant Song," and the most famous chapter on the Suffering Servant.

fallen, foolish, and malicious people. St. Paul pulls no punches in this: "For we ourselves were once foolish, disobedient, led astray, slaves to various passions and pleasures, passing our days in malice and envy, hated by men and hating one another" (Ti 3:3).

This is how God loves us: "God so loved the world that he gave his only Son, that whoever believes in him should not perish but have eternal life" (Jn 3:16). God so loved *what* world? A good world gone very bad. Jesus came to save what kind of people? The righteous? People who were already fine and good? No: "I have not come to call the righteous, but sinners to repentance" (Lk 5:32). This means you. This means me.

Does God have a clear opening into your life right now? Maybe the opening he needs is your complete inability to understand how he is loving you right now. Maybe it is your sinfulness. Maybe it is your inability to see the next step you have to take, or how to resolve a problem that seems insoluble. Let him in and let yourself be loved.

Even though the Psalms often describe God's love as unfailing or "steadfast," still we might feel like we're standing on foreign soil. Everyone knows what inconsistent, failed love is; everyone knows what it is to be loved from mixed or inferior motives. But what is it like to be loved in a consistently unfailing way?

But I have trusted in thy steadfast love;
　　my heart shall rejoice in thy salvation. (Ps 13:5)

Let thy steadfast love, O LORD, be upon us,
　　even as we hope in thee. (Ps 33:22)

Thy steadfast love, O Lord, extends to the
　　heavens,
　　thy faithfulness to the clouds. (Ps 36:5)

To be loved in a steadfast way is to be loved by One who knows the whole story about you, your entire biography, not excluding the darker and shameful points, and has still woven it all into his providence. He doesn't stop loving people even when they may stop loving themselves. Even more than comforting, this is transforming. To recognize in our lives a love that has always been there, loving us to deeper conversion and reconciliation, is the only thing that can move us to love the right things rightly—and so *run*.

The simple reason behind this? As the old saying goes: you can't give what you don't have. If we had never experienced a free love, one that gives without a "catch," one totally lacking in neediness or self-interest, how could we love God or neighbor in any kind of selfless, truly Christlike way? God himself shows us the way by loving us first, loving us best, and loving us to the end. Awakening to the presence of this love in our lives turns our hearts away from all cheap imitations, all the inferior knockoffs that we sinners use to get by. He brings us to a place where we can say with confidence: "I love the Lord" (Ps 116:1).

In concluding both this chapter and the book, a line from the liturgy suggests itself. Whenever I celebrate a requiem (or funeral) Mass, I linger over a particularly consoling line from the preface to the Eucharistic Prayer: "*Vita mutatur, non tollitur*": "Life is changed, not ended,"[15] or: *Life is changed, not taken away.*

If we were to take that verse and replace *vita* with *amor*, love, I think we would end up with a profound description of what the Holy Spirit is doing within us, what our whole conversion process encompasses, and what the entire Book of Psalms teaches us: *Amor mutatur, non tollitur*: "Love is changed, not ended, not taken away." Our love as Christians is radically changed, but not taken away. How so?

David was a man after God's own heart. The songs that flowed out of that godly heart, and out of the other psalmists who shared his spirit, are songs of a soul in transition, or in the concise Latin phrase, *in via*, on the way. He is a *viator*, a wayfarer, journeying not so much in steps or miles as in relationship with God. The Psalter is a kind of journal of developmental

---

15. "Preface I for the Dead," *The Roman Missal*, no. 78.

progress: from initial conversion to gradual justification to the unfettered praise of the redeemed and sanctified. St. Thomas Aquinas divides the entire Psalter into three thematic sections reflecting this movement: penitence, the thirst for justice and personal justification, and the praise of eternal glory. They comprise the threefold state of the spiritual life in faithful souls.[16]

In the end, the Psalter is the soul's hymnal. These are the songs of the soul's growing pains, its raptures, its confusion and distress, its agony and peace. But at each juncture, love is the bridge across which the trusting soul passes. And every prayer said, every rescue pleaded for, every mercy sought after, every cry of praise, is a chapter in the story of the soul's maturation in love—both in learning to love and in being loved. Even as the psalmist wrestles with the Lord, or cries out of desolation, or jubilantly rejoices, love empowers him to wait, to cry from the depths with the assurance of being heard, to repent with hope, to praise with abandon.

---

16. Thomas Aquinas, *In psalmos Davidis expositio, Prooemium.* To my knowledge there exists no standard English translation of St. Thomas' *Exposition on the Psalms of David*. The Latin original is available at Corpus Thomisticum: *http://www.corpusthomisticum.org/cps00.html.*

That this divine love might be in us, our affections do not need to be discarded. They need to be renewed and redirected toward the one thing necessary: *the love of God in Christ Jesus our Lord* (cf. Rm 8:39). At first, conversion demands much self-initiated cutting off, much detachment. The person puts distance between itself and morally toxic places and crowds, and other influences that endanger or wreck the life of grace within us. As fallen people, we have a lot of practice loving things that are frankly no good for us, but which we nevertheless become attached to. Still, as indispensable as this is, our transformation means less the cutting off of diseased limbs than it does stanching the outflow of our good love into bad channels. Bricking up the doors leading into "the tents of wickedness" (Ps 84:10), and throwing wide the gates to let in the King of Glory (cf. Ps 24:7–10), is the main work before us.

To borrow an image from Ecclesiastes—one used over and again in poetry and popular music: just as all streams flow to the sea, so must all of our loves turn into the one channel of God's love (cf. Eccl 1:7). They must flow into the sea of his love. That is what conversion aims at, and what holiness is. Making the Psalms of David our songbook on this journey is to allow the Lord to teach us how to pray, cry, and sing our way along the pathway of growth in Christian life and love.

I can find no better way of concluding these reflections than quoting Psalm 30 in full. All of the struggle, rapture, tears, and trust found in the entire Psalter are condensed diamond-like in these verses:

> I will extol thee, O Lord, for thou hast drawn me up,
>   and hast not let my foes rejoice over me.
> O Lord my God, I cried to thee for help,
>   and thou hast healed me.
> O Lord, thou hast brought up my soul from Sheol,
>   restored me to life from among those gone
>   down to the Pit.
>
> Sing praises to the Lord, O you his saints,
>   and give thanks to his holy name.
> For his anger is but for a moment,
>   and his favor is for a lifetime.
> Weeping may tarry for the night,
>   but joy comes with the morning.
>
> As for me, I said in my prosperity,
>   "I shall never be moved."
> By thy favor, O Lord,
>   thou hadst established me as a strong mountain;
> thou didst hide thy face,
>   I was dismayed.

To thee, O Lord, I cried;
  and to the Lord I made supplication:
"What profit is there in my death,
  if I go down to the Pit?
Will the dust praise thee?
  Will it tell of thy faithfulness?
Hear, O Lord, and be gracious to me!
  O Lord, be thou my helper!"

Thou hast turned for me my mourning into
    dancing;
  thou hast loosed my sackcloth
  and girded me with gladness,
that my soul may praise thee and not be silent.
  O Lord my God, I will give thanks to thee
    for ever.

Appendix

⁓

Strength for the Battle
Verses for Victory

For thou didst gird me with strength for the battle;
thou didst make my assailants sink under me.

—PSALM 18:39

Compilations such as the above-mentioned *Talking Back* of Evagrius of Pontus evolve out of first-hand experience of conflict. More than an index of pious invocations, verses collected from the psalms and other parts of Scripture catalogue the tactics of spiritual war heroes who have fought the good fight and discovered, if only after many wounds, the source of true strength.

Through thee we push down our foes;
> through thy name we tread down our assailants.
For not in my bow do I trust,
> nor can my sword save me.

But thou hast saved us from our foes,
    and hast put to confusion those who hate us.
    (Ps 44:5–7)

Throughout the ages, the intuition of saints (and those struggling to become saints) has invariably been to keep a personal list of psalm verses suited to their particular needs. Overwhelmed by life's challenges, bedeviled by temptations, daunted by the virulence of an enemy, and frightened by one's own weakness, souls of prayer discover in the psalms an arsenal of verses adapted to any adversity. They also find the victories the Lord enables. Songs of praise and thanksgiving crown the struggle of every persevering soul.

Such verses would naturally suggest themselves to those already accustomed to the daily recitation of the Breviary (*Liturgy of the Hours*). One cannot pray the Breviary day in and day out without alighting on words and phrases that both comfort and sustain the soul outside of times reserved for formal prayer. Having prayed the Divine Office with attention and devotion, inserting the inspired lines of the psalms into the mix of daily life comes spontaneously.

But even for those unaccustomed to the structure of the Office, regular reflection on the psalms leads to the same kind of impromptu prayer. In the athletic and martial imagery favored by the earliest monks and ascetics, as the hurling of javelins. These prayers are quick, direct, to the point, and easy to memorize. Since the early monastic fathers rightly attached great importance to the role played by one's private thoughts in the spiritual life, it is no wonder that they resorted to the psalms as an antidote against the harmful ones.

Thoughts or suggestions often lead to desires, which in their turn frequently steer us to act in good or bad ways. Since tempting thoughts disturb peace of soul and make sober thinking difficult, countering bad thoughts immediately with the truth and power of God's word is crucial. Our Lord's own words are confirmation enough:

> But what comes out of the mouth proceeds from the heart, and this defiles a man. For out of the heart come evil thoughts, murder, adultery, fornication, theft, false witness, slander. These are what defile a man. . . . (MT 15:18–20)

Total passivity is never advisable when under attack, especially when God has provided a munitions store equipping us for everything from the occasional skirmish to total war. In light of the New Testament call to arms, we cannot afford to advance weaponless into the fray:

From the days of John the Baptist until now the kingdom of heaven has suffered violence, and men of violence take it by force. (MT 11:12)

For though we live in the world we are not carrying on a worldly war, for the weapons of our warfare are not worldly but have divine power to destroy strongholds. (2 COR 10:3–4)

This charge I commit to you, Timothy, my son, in accordance with the prophetic utterances which pointed to you, that inspired by them you may wage the good warfare, holding faith and a good conscience. (1 TM 1:18–19)

Somewhat like the small pouch of smooth stones with which David slew Goliath (cf. 1 Sm 17), the following is a relatively brief and partial collection of psalm verses ready to hand both in times of war and peace, conflict and victory. It is hoped that readers will find in them inspiration to amass their own reserve of verses.

In Urgent Need or Temptation

- "Turn, O LORD, save my life;
    deliver me for the sake of thy steadfast love." (6:4)

- "Incline thy ear to me,
    rescue me speedily!

Be thou a rock of refuge for me,
 a strong fortress to save me!" (31:2)

- "[D]eliver me from those who work evil,
 and save me from bloodthirsty men." (59:2)

- "Save me, O God! For the waters have come up to my neck." (69:1)

- "Be pleased, O God, to deliver me!
 O LORD, make haste to help me!" (Ps 70:1)

Against Fear

- "The LORD is my light and my salvation;
 whom shall I fear?
The LORD is the stronghold of my life;
 of whom shall I be afraid?" (27:1)

- "When I am afraid, I put my trust in thee." (56:3)

Against Despair

- "For the needy shall not always be forgotten,
 and the hope of the poor shall not perish
  for ever." (9:18)

- "For God alone my soul waits in silence,
 for my hope is from him.
He only is my rock and my salvation,
 my fortress; I shall not be shaken." (62:5–6)

Against Lust

- "[T]he commandment of the LORD is pure,
    enlightening the eyes;
  the fear of the LORD is clean,
    enduring for ever." (19:8–9)

- Who shall ascend the hill of the LORD?
    And who shall stand in his holy place?
  He who has clean hands and a pure heart,
    who does not lift up his soul to what
      is false, . . ." (24:3–4)

Against Anger

- "But I have calmed and quieted my soul,
    like a child quieted at its mother's breast;
    like a child that is quieted is my soul." (131:2)

- "Refrain from anger, and forsake wrath!
    Fret not yourself; it tends only to evil.
  For the wicked shall be cut off;
    but those who wait for the LORD shall possess
      the land." (37:8–9)

Against Envy

- "Fret not yourself because of the wicked,
    be not envious of wrongdoers!

For they will soon fade like the grass,
    and wither like the green herb." (37:1)

In Desolation and Weakness

- "But I am poor and needy;
    hasten to me, O God!
  Thou art my help and my deliverer;
    O LORD, do not tarry!" (70:5)

- "Incline thy ear, O LORD, and answer me,
    for I am poor and needy." (86:1)

In Thanksgiving

- "I will give to the Lord the thanks due to his
    righteousness,
  and I will sing praise to the name of the LORD,
    the Most High." (7:17)

- "I will give thanks to the LORD with my whole
    heart;
  I will tell of all thy wonderful deeds." (9:1)

In Praise

- "I will be glad and exult in thee,
  I will sing praise to thy name, O Most High."
  (9:2)

- "Be exalted, O Lord, in thy strength!
    We will sing and praise thy power." (21:13)

- "Sing praises to God, sing praises!
    Sing praises to our King, sing praises!" (47:6)